in search of
HAPPINESS

John F. Schumaker is an internationally known clinical psychologist and social critic who has authored and edited nine previous books on subjects dealing with culture, cross-cultural mental health, religion, suggestibility, dissociation, and self-deception. His recent book *The Age of Insanity* explores the psychological consequences of modernisation and consumerism. Originally from Wisconsin in the USA, he has spent the last twenty-five years living and working in different countries, including Zambia, South Africa, Thailand, Great Britain, Ireland, Australia, and New Zealand.

in search of

HAPPINESS

Understanding an endangered state of mind

JOHN F. SCHUMAKER

PRAEGER

Westport, Connecticut
London

Library of Congress Cataloging in Publication Data:
Schumaker, John F., 1949–
    In search of happiness: understanding an endangered state of mind / John F.
    Schumaker.
        p. cm.
    Includes bibliographical references and index.
    ISBN 0-275-99456-2 (alk. paper)
    1. Happiness. I. Title.
    BF575.H27S38 2007
    152.4'2—dc22   2006038205

English language edition, except the United States and Canada,
published by Penguin Publishers.

First published by Penguin Group (NZ), 2006

Copyright © 2007 by John F. Schumaker

Library of Congress Catalog Card Number: 2006038205

ISBN-13: 978-0-275-99456-3
ISBN-10: 0-275-99456-2

Published in the United States and Canada by
Praeger Publishers, 88 Post Road West, Westport, CT 06881
An imprint of Greenwood Publishing Group, Inc.
www.praeger.com

Designed by Mary Egan
Typeset by Egan Reid Ltd
Printed in Australia by McPherson's Printing Group

10 9 8 7 6 5 4 3 2 1

Contents

Preface

I never thought I would find myself writing a book about happiness. Most of my latest works have dealt with darkish topics, in particular the ongoing disintegration of modern society and its institutions. My previous book *The Age of Insanity* even argues that the basic cultural blueprint guiding people today is largely insane in terms of our prospects for social and psychological well-being. Yet it occurred to me that much of what I have been writing and thinking about in recent years also has direct implications for what is happening to human happiness. I also felt that we stand to learn a great deal about happiness by looking at the 'big picture', which is the perspective that I always find most illuminating.

Most books about happiness have been written from the perspective of the individual. These often describe ways in which the person can enhance their own happiness in relation to their personal circumstances. This book was not written primarily as a self-help or how-to book, although there are strong elements of that within it. It was also not intended to limit itself to the scientific research that is beginning to appear on the subject of happiness. Nor did it set out merely to summarise the different philosophies of happiness. Instead, I opted to write about happiness in somewhat of a biographical fashion. The approach I took was to explore the whole issue of happiness in a wide historical and cultural perspective. It is a very eclectic approach that draws from multiple sources of knowledge, including psychology, sociology, anthropology, evolutionary biology, philosophy, economics, and religious studies. In so doing, I try to define the essence of happiness at various ages in the past, as well as what it has become and where it is going as a result of the current mega-forces that give direction to our lives. Several chapters are devoted to specific developments of the modern era that have redefined happiness and reshaped its experience. I even stuck my neck out and included chapters on prehistoric happiness and the future of happiness.

I confess that, when I look around me, I do not see a very happy world. This is despite the collective preoccupation with happiness, and with anything that can make people happier. The majority of people still appear to be living in ways that are not conducive to happiness. Some people will disagree with this view, pointing out that a high percentage of individuals still claim to be happy. But in my mind, we were meant to be far more social, spiritual, loving, and intellectually engaged than we are being programmed to be by modern consumer culture. This makes it very difficult to arrive at a meaningful state of happiness.

At numerous points throughout the book, I use words such as 'genuine', 'authentic', and 'deep-felt' to describe the higher grades of happiness that contrast sharply with the more superficial varieties that tend to be the consequence of contemporary consumer living. I make the point that millions of people have been sent on a wild goose chase for a type of happiness that does not nourish them at the base of their being. In doing so, many modern people are losing sight of, and neglecting important aspects of, their lives and their relationships. This will be controversial to anyone who believes that all experiences of happiness are of the same quality and durability, or that it does not matter what path one takes in achieving happiness.

I did not want to end up with a book about happiness that was depressing, even though I feel that the story of the life and death of happiness is a rather sad one. Therefore, I decided to incorporate what I feel are universal truths about, and insights into, happiness. I did this in the form of 'Happiness Keys' that are interspersed throughout the book. I use some of these as an excuse to go off on small tangents in order to compare the effectiveness of present-day happiness pathways to those employed in former times, or in different cultures. As the reader will quickly gather, many of my core assumptions and conclusions about happiness were formed as a result of my encounters with people from a diversity of cultures. I have had the privilege of living and working in a number of different countries in Africa, Asia, Europe, Australasia, as well as my native North America. I took the liberty of highlighting some discussions with descriptions of my personal experiences. These include the contact I have had with people who inhabit what I call 'happy societies'.

Despite the critical eye that is cast upon the modern formula for happiness, I hope that this is not seen as a wholesale discounting of our prospects for a happy life. I have not lost sight of the immense capacity of the human being to resurrect itself from dire situations, or in this case cultural and economic systems that are toxic to many essential human needs. I do not see the future of happiness as an entirely black one, and I grew even more hopeful as I came into contact with numerous visionaries in the course of writing this book who are actively seeking to promote more meaningful roads to happiness.

I am especially grateful to Finlay Macdonald of Penguin Books for giving me the opportunity to write this book, and for his encouragement that saw me through times of self-doubt. My appreciation also goes out to Alison Brook of Penguin Books for her valuable editorial, technical, and creative contributions. There were countless people whose wisdom and insights helped me to solidify my thinking on this exceedingly slippery topic. Among those who deserve special mention are Catherine O'Brien, Charles Hayes, Reverend Sa'ai u Ale Palelei, Ben Schumaker, and The Wizard of New Zealand. I will always owe a debt of gratitude to Charles Sontag and Mack H. Singleton, two former teachers at the University of Wisconsin who improved my destiny. Most of all, my deepest thanks to my wife Cheryl. Without her generous assistance, support, and inspiration, this book would never have become a reality.

CHAPTER ONE

Dying to Be Happy

WHEN future archaeologists sift through the layers of artefacts that were part of the current era, they are going to scratch their heads over the vast quantities of happy faces. They will find bright yellow happy faces in the form of pin-on buttons, adhesive decals, refrigerator magnets, knobs for pens and pencils, happy-face ties, coffee mugs, wallpaper, stationery, and bumper stickers. Luck might even lead them to one of the millions of happy-face stamps issued by the US Postal Service in 1999.

Debate will surely follow since human beings have never had a reputation as being particularly happy creatures. The dolphin or kea maybe, but not humans. Some will label us *homo happilus* and theorise that we lived in some sort of ideal world that kept everyone smiling. Sceptics will tag us *homo miserables* and argue to the contrary that, for some reason, we were a profoundly dismal species and our cherished happy faces were the only thing standing between us and despair. One clever archaeologist might see the happy face as the symbol for a global good-news religion. The star pupil among them might figure out that first we depleted the forests and animals, followed by the sea, then the air we breathe, and finally our own emotions.

Happiness now reigns supreme over noble priorities such as love, health, family, God, wisdom, and honesty. Get happy. The rest is icing on the cake. In surveys that ask 'What is the most important thing in life?' happiness is by far the most common answer. When people are asked what they want more than anything else, 'happiness' comes out head and shoulders above all other goals. Ask parents what they want, above all else, for their children and their answers will be the same: 'To be happy.'

Little or no tolerance remains for bad news. Books with negative-sounding words in their titles do not sell well. Personal ads presenting the person as sober and socially concerned get few replies. Positiveness, even in the face of an apocalyptic nightmare, has become so vogue that pessimists and realists have lost almost all appeal. The cheerleaders are policing the game with an iron fist. All of society's seers are at risk of being neutered by the decree of mandatory positivity. Only the bravest are not being bullied into cheering up or at least shutting up.

There is little doubt that we are taking happiness very seriously nowadays. The quest for happiness has become nothing short of a cultural obsession. Never before has our species been more preoccupied with issues of happiness, or more fearful that they might not be as happy as they could be. It is not true, as we have come to assume, that human beings naturally regard happiness as the main purpose of life, or the highest value that steers their existence. Personal happiness as an end in itself that transcends all other values and goals is quite a recent development.

There are a number of notable people who have denounced the search for happiness. Albert Einstein once said 'Happiness never appeared to me as an absolute aim. I am even inclined to compare such moral aims to the ambitions of a pig.' Some say that this pigs-at-the-trough analogy is appropriate for the way in which people today strive to slurp up happiness. In his 1903 play *Man and Superman*, George Bernard Shaw proclaimed 'A lifetime of happiness! No man alive could bear it: it would be hell on earth.' Novelist Joseph Heller once wrote in the *Observer* that 'The idea of always being blissfully happy is scary.' He imagined this hypothetical creature to be some sort of smiling vegetable. It is probably true that a nation of people who looked like those on every cover of *Happiness Across America* magazine could be taken over by a small army of ants.

Journalist Jeremy Seabrook spoke out recently about his reasons for turning against all the happiness fanfare. He writes about victims like himself of fraudulent happiness in his *Guardian* newspaper article 'For People Like Me, This Era of Insistent Jollity Is a Trial'. He describes his own temperament as 'melancholic' but not depressed, and says it is simply his nature to view the world in the wider realities of loss, decay, and misfortune. But all around him, he sees people driven to delete these realities from their experience in order to drape themselves in a veil of mirth: 'I have experienced as violence the emergence of the culture of compulsory industrialised joy, which is the companion of consumerism.' Not surprisingly, Seabrook's article was jeered immediately by angry happiness fans. One critic dismissed Seabrook's plea for understanding by accusing him of a 'cramped and joyless outlook' that celebrated misery and renounced people's right to have fun. The heat has certainly been turned up on anyone tempted to doubt the cause of happiness.

The happiness rage is revealing itself in many ways. The never-ending stream of self-help books, magazine articles, feel-good gurus, television and radio programmes, workshops, infomercial videos and DVDs, internet discussion lists and so on – all promising in their own way to fast-track us to the ultimate prize of happiness. New professions, such as happiness counselling, happiness coaching, life-lift coaching, and joyology are being invented to cope with the demand. Laughter therapy has become very popular. Those who recommend this therapy often cite studies showing that people today laugh only one-third as much as people did fifty years ago. Laughter clubs, which operate on the adage 'Fake it until you make it', are multiplying at a fast pace.

Happiness has been elevated to a must-have state of mind and everyone is selling it – film corporations, drug companies, toy manufacturers, the burgeoning body-makeover industry, theme parks, and fast-food restaurants. High-priced happiness camps and happiness retreats are popping up to meet the demand. Our colossal appetite for all things happy is turning this emotion into a 'brand', which explains curiosities such as McDonald's Happy Meals, Disneyland's official label as 'The Happiest Place on Earth', and Revlon's 'Pink Happiness' line of cosmetics. The Fisher-Price toy company promotes itself with the motto 'Happiness is a dream of Fisher-Price'. The giant discount retailer Wal-Mart – famous for their smiley-face butter cookies but infamous for destroying local communities and livelihoods – adopted the happy face in the form of a mischievous elf who flits about in commercials, knocking down prices.

Happiness is being marketed to death. Forget sex. It is the number-one result that advertisers want to associate with their products. Business establishments of every variety are riding the happiness wave. A tour through Los Angeles – sometimes dubbed the feel-good capital of the universe – will take you past Happy Donuts, Happy Liquor, Happy World Baby Clothes, Happy Day Care, Happy Shoes, Happy Trails Pet Services, Happy Couple Marriage Centre, Happy Dental Centre, and hundreds of other happy businesses. Of course it is not just Los Angeles. In Switzerland, for instance, their newest and biggest amusement park is called Happyland New.

Some doubters of the rise of all things happy say that this is just another of today's many 'bubbles', born of a society bouncing around between extremes, and not too unlike the irrational stock market or property bubbles of recent years. They feel it is just a matter of time before this emotional bubble bursts and we once again resign ourselves to being joyless consumers. But the irrational exuberance surrounding happiness appears to be more than the emotional equivalent of the hula hoop or bell-bottom jeans. Large cultural shifts have taken place that have redefined happiness and given it a new significance, and a new role in people's lives.

Growing numbers of university academics are throwing their hats into the ring and helping to legitimise the cultural love affair with happiness. A branch of psychology, known as Happiness Studies, has emerged, and the year 1999 saw the debut of the *Journal of Happiness Studies*. Researchers from around the world are publishing their work, not only in this journal, but in a wide range of other publications that would not have touched this topic ten years ago. Courses titled 'The Psychology of Happiness' and 'The Science of Happiness' are being introduced in universities and continuing-education centres all over the world.

Privately run happiness institutes are becoming big business. Often headed by positive psychologists who seem to inevitably attract the nickname 'Dr Happy', they can command high prices for their various 'happiness services'. Some of them make claims that happiness has enough muscle to defuse modern maladies such as depression, obesity, stress, and insomnia. Most of these institutes have close corporate ties, and promise that happiness can promote business success and increase worker satisfaction.

Happiness has become the dominant illusion of the modern age. Even if people know what makes them happy, most are racked with self-doubt. Their expectations for happiness have become greatly magnified. They are not sure how much is enough. With the happiness crusade reaching fever pitch, it is easy to get the impression that nothing whatsoever is holding us back from happiness on a grand or even celestial scale.

But becoming as happy as it appears we can be is a daunting prospect. It takes real determination, for example, to wade through a book like David Burns's 732-page *Feeling Good Handbook*, a blockbuster that has sold over two million copies. Inside the front cover is a litany of rave reviews by readers, including one that says 'It's my Bible', which proves that many people are in fact willing to do the hard yards to reach their goal of happiness. Likewise, many purchasers of the mechanical step-by-step guides to happiness are willing to wrestle with daily mood charts, happy thought diaries, and good feeling logs as they forge on toward their dream of happiness. When it comes to happiness, people are really thinking big.

We have entered uncharted emotional territory. What is certain is that we are no longer talking about the ordinary happiness that naturally punctuates the emotional worlds of people as they go about the task of living. Instead, people are setting their sights on supercharged happiness. Our hopes for happiness are being pumped up continually, with the promise of achieving pot-boiling happiness as a total way of life.

Books abound with such titles as *Perfect Happiness*, *Infinite Happiness*, *Maximum Happiness*, and *Absolute Happiness*. It has reached the point where it is common to ask 'Do you believe in happiness?', a sign that today's brand of happiness is akin to Santa Claus and the Tooth Fairy. The adage 'One can never be too rich or too thin' seems to have been revised to include 'can never be too happy'. Or can one?

Research actually shows that people whose happiness comes in intense bursts tend to be prone to mood swings in the opposite direction. The healthy brain seems to resist letting moods go too far in either direction, which makes a mockery of the 'infinite happiness' fabrications being propagated by the happiness industry. Yet the concept of happiness has become so hallowed that it is beginning to resemble a cult or religious surrogate. The way in which some folks express the significance of happiness certainly sounds like religion, with the happy person often portrayed as someone who has attained a sort of omnipotence. Some happiness zealots are slipping into an evangelical 'us' versus 'them' mentality, with happiness being the salvation that comes when one admits to the sin of unhappiness and follows the rules of redemption set out by the chosen (i.e. happy) people.

Happiness clubs are attracting growing numbers of emotion-seekers. They represent a new form of spiritual congregation that reinforces the sacredness of happiness and hails it as a force that can exile the whole world from unhappiness. Recently, the president of the popular International Happiness Club wrote on their website that the dedicated missionaries of happiness are making progress: 'There are more and more happy people all the time. It is catching on fast. It may become an epidemic if you begin being happy right now.' On the power and invincibility of happy people, he added, 'Don't mess with a happy person, you have no way of controlling them or making them react to negative things.' Happiness is on the march and advancing us toward what he calls 'the greatness of a real community'.

Happiness is even becoming the stuff of which miracles are made. One life-lift coach recently attributed the dramatic improvement in her previously untreatable glaucoma condition to the elevated happiness that she managed to achieve by way of her particular programme. Among the swelling ranks of happiness coaches are those who present themselves as spiritual guides of one type or another. For example, one professional happiness coach advertises herself in the following manner:

> I am a Positive Psychologist and a Happiness Coach. What do we all want? MORE HAPPINESS, PLEASE! And how do we get it? We get it by discovering our ENCHANTED SELVES. I am here to help you do that.

She goes on to say that this seat of happiness, the Enchanted Self, is not a real place, yet one that can let people fly if it is sufficiently nourished: 'This place – this mind/body/heart within ourselves – holds within it all the Gateways to Happiness that we will ever need.' Such a blend of happiness psychology and spirituality is selling exceptionally well. A number of coaches are also marketing ongoing happiness lifeline services that give the client the impression that the coach is always there as a sort of happiness guardian. One California-based coach offers happiness 'Check-up packages' for an extra $US250 per month that bestows upon the person a couple of thirty-minute phone calls and limited email consultation. For an additional $US500 per month, you get the ultimate happiness plan that 'guides people every step of the way', which in this case means a fifteen-minute phone call every second day and unlimited emails. What we are seeing here is the birth of professional 'happiness angels'.

The stratospheric heights to which feel-good society has elevated the concept of happiness has some critics worried that, if it were to become reality, we could end up with hordes of people who are too happy for their own good or that of society. The idea of someone being too happy seems absurd on the surface, but one must wonder just how happy today's seekers want to become. When, if ever, would they step off the 'happiness treadmill', as it is sometimes called?

A number of books have appeared in recent years using cases of 'extremely happy' people to guide us to the outer limits of the happy sphere. They point out that happiness extremes can be reached through focusing one's goals, creating a dream list, learning to identify one's desires, exploring options, cultivating 'success intelligence', learning to communicate, and figuring out how to extract the most from each day. Since none of these seem excruciatingly difficult, logic tells us that a society of extremely happy people is not total science fiction.

Some people who worry that happiness is getting out of hand say that such extreme happiness would constitute a serious social disease. They reason that there is an optimal level of happiness and that excesses can take a toll on critical thinking, judgement, and curiosity. At the far reaches of happiness, they say, we even become unfit from a survival standpoint.

In a *Journal of Happiness Studies* article titled 'Are the Very Happy Too Happy?', Elisha Tarlow Friedman and her colleagues pose the question 'Is there some point beyond which the energy, enthusiasm, and sociability normally associated with happiness would give way to smug complacency, obnoxious arrogance, and lack of motivation?' They added that 'determining that too much happiness is bad for us could have alarming societal implications in an age during which average levels of happiness are very high in most cultures'.

So are we verging on an epidemic of positive emotional obesity? These researchers carried out a complex State of Mind (SOM) study to determine whether people with 'excessively positive' states of mind suffered coping problems under certain experimental conditions. In the end, they concluded 'there is nothing wrong with the high levels of happiness in present day society'. But they caution that we should not let down our guard since 'it is still not established how much more happiness will be too much'.

The message that we usually get from self-help books and the media is that we are not happy enough and that there is a lot we can do to be happier. Statistics are thrown at us to back this up. For example, one large-scale study by the University of Chicago's National Opinion Research Centre found that the percentage of Americans who report being 'very happy' dropped from 35 per cent in 1957 to 30 per cent in 1988. That does not sound good. Sociologists have even begun using the term 'unhappy consciousness' to describe the collective mood of contemporary times. Most people are convinced that happiness is becoming scarce. Thus it does not compute easily when we hear some scholars saying that, not only are we highly happy now, but that we could be on the verge of slipping into a happiness la-la land.

In trying to explain all this, some people have claimed that modern Western society is making people happier and unhappier at the same time. Maybe it produces a type of happiness in one or more areas of life that is corrosive to their chances of happiness in other areas. For instance, many of the 'happy' Western societies have rather low levels of social happiness, which could be the result of achieving high levels of self-centred material happiness. Likewise, high levels of amoral hedonistic happiness could come at the expense of spiritual happiness.

A closer look at the happiness statistics reveals that there is a lot of happiness of some sort around. In the United States, for example, which does not rank as the happiest country in the world, only 8 per cent of people describe themselves as 'not very happy' or 'not at all happy' when asked to answer the question 'Taking all things together, would you say you are: very happy; quite happy; not very happy; or not at all happy?'

When happiness is measured in terms of 'life satisfaction', only 2 per cent of Americans score below the neutral score of five when asked to rate their satisfaction with life on a scale from zero to ten. The average score is 7.5 out of ten, with the most frequent score being eight out of ten.

Such findings have led some happiness researchers to jump to the conclusion that most people are happy most of the time. Instead of an epidemic of unhappiness, maybe there is a super-abundance of happiness. There certainly seems to be a huge amount of it out there, at least given the way we are now measuring happiness. If we are on the threshold of becoming too happy, the battalion of happiness helpers out there need to eliminate this possibility before continuing their efforts to make us even happier. Or are these sorts of statistics describing something that is not actually happiness?

What Is It?

THE cultural anointment of hyper-happiness is curious in light of the intolerance that we tend to have for glaring displays of happiness from others. We are even quick to see excessive happiness as a sign of madness. Old film archives are filled with portrayals of lunatics whose main symptoms are unceasing laughter and constant bliss. We have heard the terms 'hysterical laughter' and 'hysterical happiness' and most of us have witnessed an instance of someone whose peals of laughter gradually dissolved into tears. The terms 'bomb-happy' and 'flak-happy' described a reaction to prolonged wartime bombardment.

The word 'happy' can even be used to suggest that someone has left reality behind. For instance, at a recent cocktail party, I overheard someone say 'She's gone a bit happy with her collagen injections.' As a species, we seem to have an innate capacity to detect others who are happy in a way that is out of kilter with what would be expected under prevailing circumstances. A prehistoric hunting team, ready to take on mastodons while watching out for sabre-toothed tigers, would certainly send back to the cave a member who could not stop smiling. Not many potential employers would hire an applicant who wore a permanent grin throughout the entire job interview. The saying 'Beware the smile on the face of the jury foreman' even reflects how unexplainable happiness can spook onlookers.

The happiness phenomenon is also interesting in light of the extreme and worsening epidemic of depression sweeping the Western world. One could be forgiven for asking if this is part of a collective cover-up campaign. The phrase 'smiling depression' is sometimes used to describe the way in which some people use happiness signals, such as a smile or feigned laughter, to disguise their underlying depression. The appearance of happiness can give a completely false impression of the person's inner world. Maybe what seems to be happiness is not happiness at all, but rather a reminder that we are sinking even further into the Age of Depression.

Depression is one of the grimmest trends in the Western world. The rate of this disorder has risen ten-fold over the past five decades. There has been a similar rise in 'subclinical depression' in which people show clear signs of the disorder but have not yet descended into full clinical depression. Estimates of the percentage of people who suffer from either clinical or subclinical depression range from 15 to 30 per cent, a figure that is roughly the same for most modern Western nations. Headlines were made recently by a large-scale study in New Zealand showing that 42 per cent of women were either suffering from clinical depression or had been treated for it. Similar findings coming out of other countries have raised fears that the pace of this epidemic is ever increasing, and that depression will be the social norm within the next couple of decades.

We usually assume that depression is the opposite of happiness and that a depressed person would not claim to be happy. To some extent this is true. Also, the cultural conditions that breed depression will also predispose people toward unhappiness. But the picture gets a bit confusing, which reflects certain differences between unhappiness and depression. It is frequently the case that depressed people will say that they feel unhappy, especially when the depression is acute. Those on the brink of suicide, for example, are not going to describe themselves as happy. The exception to this is the paradoxical happiness that can overcome a person who finally makes the decision to end his or her life, which is actually one of the signs to look out for in high-risk individuals. That aside, the problem is that there are more depressed people than unhappy ones.

The depression statistics do not seem to match up with the results of happiness surveys. The discrepancy is especially great in some 'happy' countries. In Sweden, for instance, only 4 per cent of people report being 'not very happy' or 'not at all happy'. At the same time, Sweden is dealing with the same plague of depression afflicting the rest of the Western world, plus its suicide rate is nearly double that of the world average.

A few different theories have been ventured to explain why depression and happiness can coexist. One of them says that happiness and depression are opposite ends of the same pole and that happy-but-depressed people are simply less happy than they realise, or are willing to admit. To admit to unhappiness in our feel-good society is tantamount to broadcasting that one is a loser. Asking someone if they are happy prompts the same defensive reaction as 'Did you have a good time on your vacation?' As awful as the vacation might have been, it is very difficult to confess it, and most people end up distorting the truth. Pointing out to a person 'You don't seem very happy' strikes as much terror as a reference to someone's bad breath. Nowadays, no effort is spared to cover up any scent of unhappiness on oneself.

With happiness carrying so much cultural clout, responses to the question 'Are you happy?' follow the same statistical pattern as the question 'Are you intelligent?' In studies that ask people to rate their own intelligence, only 2 per cent of people rate themselves as below average. Americans in particular feel intense pressure to say 'I'm fine' when asked how they are doing, no matter how miserable they might be. We do not want others to see us, or to see ourselves, as unhappy. All around us are cues and messages telling us that we need to be happy in order to be socially acceptable. This biasing effect is often not taken into account by researchers who conclude that most people have 'above neutral' levels of happiness.

There may also be a biological explanation for our ability to mask unhappiness. Research shows that our brains have an automatic tendency to forget unhappy events more quickly than happy ones. The consequence would be that, at any point in time, the person is remembering less unhappiness than happiness. This could translate into the illusion that one is happier than would be expected if happy and unhappy components were remembered equally. Such a device is a useful prophylactic against a build-up of negative emotion, and allows the person to cope in less than optimal environments.

The 'forgotten' material that would otherwise contribute to the experience of unhappiness is not completely erased. Instead, it is probably dissociated, which means it still exists as information but has been shunted outside of conscious awareness. This raises the intriguing possibility that someone can be unhappy without really knowing it. Such a prospect might explain why so many people who live under depressing conditions, and who are even on the verge of descending into a serious state of depression, can continue to perceive themselves as happy.

Those who argue that depression is not the negative end of the happiness scale sometimes point out that women suffer from depression at twice the rate of men, and yet are equal to men when it comes to measures of happiness. This is one of the reasons that some mental health professionals try to explain major depression in terms of genetics. Another is the moderately strong correlation in depression among identical twins. Gene 5-HTT has even been called the 'depressive gene'.

Many happiness researchers are quick to generalise from the genetics of depression and suggest that happiness levels are determined primarily by our genes. Some have speculated that as much as 80 per cent of happiness is the result of genetics. However, as compelling as the genetic arguments seem on the surface, they can easily fall apart when one starts looking across cultures and noting huge differences that can only be explained socially. For instance, there are a great many societies that have no anorexia nervosa whatsoever, a fact that shoots down the strictly genetic theory of that disorder. Also, a number of anthropologists have studied depression across cultures and concluded that depression is a culture-bound syndrome limited mostly to Western societies. Again this casts doubt on strictly biological theories. As will become apparent in this book, happiness also has far too large a socio-cultural component for it to be spoken of primarily in terms of genetics and biology.

Our culture is our fate to a much greater extent than most people are able to perceive.

Still another reason why depression and happiness can coexist may have to do with the consequences of modernisation and the growth of wealth. For various reasons, increasing rates of mental problems, including depression, seem to be an inevitable consequence of these developments, even though they are a source of happiness for large segments of the society. Sometimes this is called the 'modern person syndrome'. But it could be that the type of happiness that is manufactured in the course of expanding prosperity ultimately removes people from more basic and natural sources of happiness.

It needs to be kept in mind that the growing preoccupation with personal happiness is bound up with the self-absorption that has come to shape people's identity and their understanding of what it means to feel good. As people have retreated into themselves, happiness has become somewhat autistic in the way it is defined and experienced. Increasingly, it has become a private affair. In the process, many things that make one feel good by way of direct engagement with the outside world have lost an association with happiness. For example, states of awe, reverence, fascination, and empathy can feel extremely good. But all of these are interactive or shared. We sometimes no longer feel that these are happy experiences since happiness now tends to be comprehended as something that is ours and ours alone.

As odd as it sounds, the high levels of self-absorbed happiness that exist today may be driving people crazy, as well as promoting some degree of underlying unhappiness. Repression and depression are closely related. At its most basic level, genuine happiness is unity with one's nature, which is essentially a social and spiritual nature. It could be that the dehumanised variety of happiness that people chase today in consumer culture requires them to repress certain emotions and basic human tendencies that make this type of happiness depressing. This again might cause depression to be generated along with happiness. That being the case, it raises the peculiar possibility that some formats for happiness may be emotionally unfriendly to the person, and maybe even to society as a whole.

Attempts to define happiness show that it can mean many different things. It has been approached from many standpoints. These include life satisfaction, positive mental health, subjective well-being, quality of life, flow, meaning, optimism, zest, successfulness, self-esteem, hedonistic enjoyment, self-actualisation, and so on. Many of these are overlapping, and some are contradictory to others.

It does not help that the words 'happy' and 'happiness' have become so overused and debased that it is difficult to set boundaries on the concept. They have spilled over into the banal world of commodities, services, tastes, and preferences. The same has happened with other words, such as 'love' and 'excellence'. Just as we have no trouble swallowing a comment such as 'I love my car', we do not baulk upon hearing 'I am happy with my cell phone.'

There are currently around twenty different academic definitions of happiness. Quite a few academics have opted for the definition of happiness as 'the overall enjoyment of one's life as-a-whole'. But the concept of enjoyment strikes others as a less than ideal canvas on which to paint a picture of human happiness. Those who argue for a deeper appreciation of happiness claim that enjoyment models do not get at many of the core elements that lead to the most enriching types of happiness.

The 'Life Satisfaction Scale' is one of the most widely used scientific measures of happiness. It consists of five items that ask people to what extent they agree or disagree that they have gotten the important things in life; that they would change almost nothing if they could do it over again; that the conditions of life are excellent; and that life is close to ideal. One item simply asks outright if the person is satisfied with life.

But the happiness-as-satisfaction model flies in the face of historical wisdom about the need to limit satisfaction in order to lay the foundation for happiness. In other words, one can be too satisfied for one's own good. Too much of it can even lead to numbness and insensibility, which may be why Spanish painter Salvador Dali complained 'There are days when I think I'm going to die from an overdose of satisfaction.' Prescriptions for the art of living often speak of the need to ration satisfaction in order to remain fully alive and open to happiness.

Happiness Key

Happiness is a way station
between too little and too much.

— CHANNING POLLOCK

There is an ever-present tendency for us to look in a linear way at the factors that are thought to make us happy. If something makes me happy, more of that thing should make me even happier. But in the wise words of Channing Pollock, which appear in his 1928 play *Mr Moneypenny*, happiness tends to loiter in the 'way station', or switching station, between too much and too little, where a person's awareness shifts back and forth across the line of deprivation and satisfaction. It is no coincidence that the societies with the highest percentage of 'very happy' people tend to have 'life satisfaction' scores in the middle ranges. The importance of rationing satisfaction was understood by Aesop, the sixth-century BC Greek fabulist, who wrote 'We would often be sorry if our wishes were satisfied.' Wishes usually make us happier when they remain wishes.

The prospect of extremes of satisfaction even begin to muster up images of sadness. In fact, the word 'satisfaction' itself comes from the same Indo-European root as the word 'sad'. In Middle English, 'sad' carried the meaning of being glutted, satisfied, and drained. To be satisfied was, in a sense, to be sad or at least tired due to satiation, which is a far cry from most meanings of happiness. The ancient Latin proverb *post coitum comne animal trist est* – 'after intercourse every animal is sad' – is meant to convey the feeling of deflation that results from the consummation of all forms of desire. Being unsatisfied, which is not the same thing as being dissatisfied, has long been known to be a stimulant to happiness.

Today, the word 'satisfaction' creates confusion even when it is not intended to mean that happiness comes from having a full belly of one sort or another. It denotes completion and carries the connotation of someone who has arrived somewhere, whether that be a satisfactory place, level, or frame of mind. This is sometimes seen as a static state that interferes with the ongoing growth and development of the person.

We often speak of 'needs' that are embedded within human nature, which is certainly correct. But it is a mistake to assume that happiness requires these needs to be fully quenched. It seems ludicrous, for example, to say that someone's need for intellectual stimulation has been completely satisfied. What does contribute to a person's happiness is that he or she is exercising their intellect, and living in accord with that need.

The difference between exercising one's needs and satisfying them is a big one. This is why anthropologist Jean-Jacques Rousseau phrased the good life as 'existing according to one's intrinsic potentiality of one's nature'. The full satisfaction of our needs can actually be a major obstacle to happiness.

Another problem with viewing happiness in light of being satisfied concerns what is actually being satisfied. Consumer culture has a way of filling people with false needs while disconnecting them from essential human needs that are more conducive to true happiness. It may be that these false needs get complete satisfaction, which could even lead the person to report feeling satisfied. But this type of satisfaction could offer nothing in terms of real happiness, and might even block access to it. Several factors that we often associate with happiness can also become toxic in excessive quantities. As we will see later, these include success, self-esteem, ambition, and personal power.

Relativism dominates our current thinking about happiness. This means that we do not make judgements about the quality of a person's supposed happiness, or how he or she got to be happy in the first place. So long as someone says 'I'm happy', it does not matter if he or she got that way by fighting poverty, selling seal pup pelts, collecting Smurf toys, or leading a skinhead gang. In fact, happiness comes in many colours, shapes, and sizes. Some types are fragile and will crumble easily, while others have deeper root systems that make them more enduring and deeply felt.

All modes of happiness are an extension of a person's values. It is only possible to understand happiness in relation to these values and the ideals that follow from them. In this regard, one of the best definitions of happiness is given by novelist Ayn Rand: 'Happiness is that state of consciousness which proceeds from the achievement of one's values.' This changes the question 'What makes you happy?' to 'What are your values?' When asked about their happiness, people automatically filter their answers through the values that have been instilled in them by their culture.

Sometimes the key values of a society, as well as the primary means for happiness, are revealed in the greetings and well-wishings that people give one another. In traditional Mongolian society, for instance, people would say to one another 'Your animals are fattening up nicely', or bid them adieu with the hopes that the animals would get fat. Many native societies of North America tended to wish each other beauty. Their counterpart of 'Have a nice day' was 'May you always walk in beauty'. They tended to see the Europeans as peculiarly impoverished when it came to the skill of living beautifully. The way of the Europeans seemed ugly and unnecessarily destructive, especially regarding their relationship to the natural world. This was diametrically opposed to all of their wisdom about a beautiful life.

Happiness Key

We travel through life
Searching for the beautiful,
But unless we carry it with us as we go,
We will never find it.

– RALPH WALDO EMERSON

The above words by Emerson are a treasure for a number of reasons. They set out the search for beauty as an ideal value upon which to navigate one's life. More importantly, Emerson gets to the heart of what it takes to actually find beauty, as well as happiness. As we journey through life, it is not enough merely to pluck and discard the beauty that crosses our path. We must take it into ourselves, walk with it, and become it. We do not find beauty until we ourselves become beautiful.

The Navajo people of the Southwestern United States use the word Hózhó to describe the beauty that receives top priority within that society. But Hózhó goes far beyond the passive recognition of beauty outside of oneself. It is understood as the highest form of consciousness and the ultimate goal of human destiny. Hózhó carries the additional meaning of harmony, order, equilibrium, and balance, all of which are seen as essential elements of happiness and universal well-being. For the Navajo, one does not find beauty, just as one does not find happiness. One enters into beauty by firstly creating it, and then incorporating it into oneself. In a similar vein to Emerson, one achieves beauty by becoming beautiful. The Navajo might also say that one becomes happy only when one becomes happiness itself. It is an active process that requires individuals to develop themselves to the fullest, and to become fountains from which happiness flows out to the rest of the world.

The reason why happiness is so much more cultural than biological is that the values underpinning happiness are largely a byproduct of cultural learning. These vary enormously from one culture to the next, with the partial exception of culturally universal values such as religion, marriage, and family. Most members act on their culturally installed values without questioning them to any significant degree. The vast majority of people within any society will think of themselves as happy if their lives match up with the values that are the product of their cultural indoctrination.

Conversely, people learn about cultural taboos that they believe will detract from happiness and make them unacceptable to the society. Air-cushioned Nike shoes and limited edition jeans are complete duds for the supremely happy Buddhist lama who got that way by the renunciation of earthly possessions. Nuggets of wisdom are equally useless ammunition for materialists on the hunt for consumer happiness.

In the West, coming first is a primary value. Being last is assumed to be the same thing as being unhappy. So self-reports of happiness will be influenced by the extent to which a person feels that he or she is leading or lagging behind the pack. By contrast, traditional African and Asian cultures emphasise social responsibility and cooperation. As it turns out, the quest to be the first is the prime source of the social alienation that is blamed for the rapidly deteriorating mental health of the modern Western person.

The term 'values pollution' is sometimes used to describe the sick values that are circulating in consumer society. When values become too polluted, a person can easily become condemned to an inferior, precarious, and fleeting happiness that only feels like happiness because it somehow coincides with the prevailing values of the culture. We do not usually think in terms of the fitness or lack of fitness of a culture. But cultures are capable of developing catastrophic flaws, including those that impact on the happiness of its members. In peeking behind the facade of the happy face, one quickly sees that we now live in a culture of unhappiness. Being happy within it is no guarantee that one has found a healthy format for happiness.

Psychologist Erich Fromm is known for his theory that

cultures can produce 'adjusted' people who at a deep human level are highly maladjusted. It allows us to say that, in a society that has become insane in terms of the fundamental human design, there is a strong chance that a culturally conforming 'happy' person is actually quite miserable at heart. In his book *The Sane Society*, Fromm writes that the happiness and adjustment of modern consumer sucklings are only skin deep. Look more closely, he says, and what you see is 'a society of notoriously unhappy, lonely, anxious, depressed, destructive and dependent people who are glad when we have killed the time we are trying to save'. Fromm goes on to describe an alternative social order that, unlike consumer culture which is toxic to all of our core 'existential needs', would encourage us once again to live in accordance with our human design. He even felt that the healthiest people in a society as sick as the one that exists today in the West are more likely to feel unhappy and abnormal. His greatest worries were for the 'happy' people.

Sometimes happiness seems to break all the rules. It can even dwell in the things that hold the greatest potential for suffering. For instance, few of life's endeavours give me more happiness than writing. Yet it delivers equal quantities of torment and frustration. This does not deter me; in fact, it can ultimately enhance the attraction of the process. Often the most powerfully moving activities are ones that serve the person at a more fundamental level than what we think of today as happiness. Some types of happiness – possibly the most profoundly gratifying ones – are not dependent on positive outlook, jolliness, or comfort.

The notion that there are different types of happiness can actually help us to understand a good deal of what is going on today with all the happiness hype, including why happiness and depression are such intimate bedfellows, and why the appetite for the present type of happiness is often insatiable and compulsive. Sometimes we hear the phrase 'happy in love' which we could take to mean that the person's need for love is being addressed. We could also speak of 'material happiness' in the sense of an individual's material needs are being attended to effectively. One could even say that there are as many types of happiness as there are human needs. This would also let us talk about spiritual happiness, intellectual happiness, social happiness, sexual happiness, and so forth.

One issue that would arise from this would be the balance that people have in terms of the happiness within different areas of their lives. Are they happy across the full spectrum of their needs? Or does one dominate to the exclusion of others, which is often said to be the case in consumer culture where happiness is far too concentrated in the domain of objects and self-indulgences? In his book *Happiness is Overrated*, Raymond Belliotti uses the term 'worthwhile happiness' to describe a happiness that is more kosher than what he calls the 'machine-produced happiness' of today in which we are reduced to a vacuous blob of sensations. By worthwhile happiness, he means an abiding sense that accompanies a 'positive evaluation that we are leading meaningful and valuable lives', while pursuing important projects and activities beyond the self. This differs greatly from the fleeting desirable emotions that many modern consumers have come to equate with happiness.

Any conclusions that are drawn about happiness must first take into account the actual state, or health, of happiness that exists within a society. The same is true when one tries to gauge other traits. Take religion, for example. Around 95 per cent of Americans report that they believe in God, and a high percentage describe themselves as 'quite religious' or 'very religious'. If we took this at face value, we would simply conclude that America is an intensely religious nation. However, the overall strength of religious conviction there has dropped dramatically over the decades, and is quite low by contrast to many non-Western societies. For Americans to say that they are 'quite religious' could easily mean nothing more than an occasional appearance at church and, if asked, an intellectual acknowledgement that God exists. Even someone claiming to be 'highly religious' would seem only half-heartedly religious when compared to a 'highly religious' person in India or West Africa, where the state of religion is far more robust.

Similarly, in light of the way in which love of others has given way to self-devotion, it no longer means much for people to say that they are 'quite in love' or 'very in love' with their spouses. As with religion, a great many people are just going through the motions of love, without much conviction or dedication. Today the masses of 'in love' people are lucky to see each other on a regular basis, and even luckier to avoid a breakup.

Happiness, like religion and love, exists today in a watered-down form and must be understood in the context of decline. The modern person finds it difficult to experience any emotion at a very deep level. In most cases, their sense of being happy is a false and fabricated one. To say 'I'm quite happy' in the current emotional climate can mean almost nothing from the vantage point of a valid and rewarding happiness.

It is no coincidence that most Western people do not seem to be happy, just as lovers no longer show much love and religious people no longer show much religion. Happiness is not what it used to be, or what it could be. Being 'very happy' does not even prevent one from being very disturbed. Some social critics describe a 'negative happiness' that seems to have emerged from the jaws of consumer culture. It is legitimate to ask if the relentless quest for this type of happiness is backfiring and becoming the source of unhappiness and even depression for some people.

There is an air of desperation about the modern plea for happiness. The sheer size and intensity of it suggests a huge vacuum which people are trying to fill. The existing quick-fix solutions do not seem to be doing the job. To understand what happiness has become, as well as the type of happiness that people today are hunting, it helps to look at it from an historical perspective. Only then can we begin to appreciate the complex social, cultural, physical, and spiritual tapestry in which genuine happiness is embedded.

CHAPTER THREE

Happiness by Design

RECENTLY there was a fascinating court case in California about the happiness of cows. It had to do with the California Milk Board's deceitful 'happy cow' advertising campaign that showed pampered-looking cows grazing blissfully in a lush grassy fairyland. The ads bragged 'Great cheese comes from happy cows. Happy cows come from California.' Since the reality is that these dairy cows typically wallow in disgusting lots that are covered with mud, urine and faeces, without a blade of grass or natural vegetation in sight, PETA (People for the Ethical Treatment of Animals) filed a lawsuit against the California government on the grounds of false advertising. They claimed that the cows were actually very unhappy. As it turned out, the case was dismissed on the grounds that false advertising laws do not apply to the government. But the judge admitted that the cows living under those conditions were probably unhappy.

Happiness is not limited to human beings, and happiness itself does not require great intelligence. When the conditions are favourable, many animals seem to show signs of happiness.

Anyone who denies the possibility that a dog can be happy has never had one, or has not treated the dog properly. A young rhinoceros in the wild will even kick up its heels and jump in apparent joy. It feels good to feel alive. If anything, throwing a lot of brain power at happiness will only chase it away. Before we felt the need to compartmentalise happiness, we were probably happy. It was part of our being.

Happiness Key

If you want to be happy, be.

— Leo Tolstoy

Happiness should not require a midwife or artificial inducement. In trying to artificially coax a state of happiness, all you usually end up with is an artificial happiness. As Tolstoy was saying, the mere state of being contains the properties that give birth to spontaneous happiness, or what is sometimes called 'inherent happiness', or 'native happiness'. There is little truth in the popular belief that happiness is a complex puzzle that needs lots of effort to figure out and achieve. A great many of earth's creatures will experience happiness as long as they are allowed to express their design. Oppositely, happiness would be difficult for a cheetah without room to run, a rhesus monkey without other rhesus monkeys, or a groundhog without ground, as is the case in some cruel zoos.

The starting point in learning about our own happiness is to ask if we are living according to our natural design. Or are we part of a zoo? At a cocktail party several years ago, a psychologist colleague of mine came up to me and remarked that I was looking a bit flat. Before I could defend myself against that charge of emotional treason, she blurted out 'What you've got to do is get in touch with the animal in you.' But the animal can get buried so far that it is difficult to retrieve.

Maybe all true happiness begins with a basic animal happiness in which the animal, including the human animal, is allowed to be true to its species-specific makeup. But arrogance on our part has tempted us on many occasions to reject the notion that we have a nature in the animal sense. Under the philosophical reign of behaviourism, this idea was especially taboo for the second half of the twentieth century. However, in recent years it has staged a comeback, and has begun to influence current theories of happiness. New lines of research are providing fresh insights into the minds and emotions of early people. This also helps us to understand our essential nature by viewing it in the longest possible historical perspective.

We usually imagine that the lives of our early ancestors were so dangerous and difficult that there was little room for happiness. They are depicted in films and other forms of media as frazzled, brutal, glassy-eyed, and always hungry. But a completely opposite picture has emerged over the past twenty years as a result of new discoveries and better research methods. Our pre-civilised ancestors existed in groups of between fifty and one hundred people, often said to be the intended size of human survival groups. They had very close kinship ties, and a strong network of cooperation and social support that was essential to their survival. They were efficient and well adapted to their environments. They needed no concept of happiness.

It is now widely accepted that pre-civilised hunter-gatherers were well fed, nutritionally healthy, intelligent, and resourceful. On the basic issue of diet, our usual image is that Palaeolithic people were physically stunted and mentally short-changed due to insufficient food or a diet that lacked adequate nutrition.

But the fossil evidence paints an opposite picture. They ate what we were meant to eat as human beings. Their diet was actually so healthy that it probably had beneficial consequences for both physical and emotional health. Likewise, they received lots of physical exercise throughout the course of their daily activities, none of which were abbreviated by conveniences and technology.

There is little doubt that diet, nutrition, and exercise contribute to one's potential for experiencing positive emotion. Many nutritionists preach that the modern diet has a negative impact on the body as well as the mind. The increased importance that people are attaching to diet as a road to inner well-being can be seen in the steady stream of articles and diet books offering 'recipes for happiness' and tips on how to 'eat your way to health and happiness'.

What is especially interesting is that many nutritionists have come to realise that the healthiest of all possible diets is the one eaten by our Palaeolithic ancestors. Large numbers of health-conscious people are turning to various 'Palaeo-diets' and 'Stone Age diets'. Among other things, Palaeolithic nutrition offered an enormous amount of variety. Hunter-gatherers were not primarily meat eaters, as was once thought. Between eighty and one hundred different wild plants, fruits, and legumes were part of their diet. In light of the large non-meat component of their diets, some historians say that it would be more accurate to refer to these early people as gatherer-hunters, rather than hunter-gatherers. In either case, they certainly had a better dietary recipe for happiness than today's eaters of processed, preserved, and modified mush.

Our improved understanding of Palaeolithic life has reignited the old 'happy savage' argument, except without use of the derogatory word 'savage'. A number of scholars have even been willing to speculate that pre-civilised people were a genuinely happier lot than those who inhabit the modern 'dead zone of civilisation', as primitivist John Zerzan calls it.

Primitivism refers to a radical philosophy that views civilisation and 'progress' as the main culprits for most of the social, psychological, and environmental ills plaguing the contemporary world. While still limited to the cultural fringes, the rising popularity of eco-primitivism has drawn more attention to this school of thought in recent years.

Eco-primitivists feel that the only way out of the environmental madness of modern social systems is to push for a truly 'deep ecology', which means a return to the ecologically sustainable lifestyles of pre-civilised tribal cultures. They rarely mean this in a literal way, but rather one that would involve a dismantling of the worst-offending social structures. On the subject of happiness, eco-primitivists argue that one cannot, or should not, be happy while participating in the wholesale destruction of nature. Instead, happiness that resonates with the human spirit is only possible in the context of living in harmony with the natural world. Nothing deserves to be called happiness if it contributes to the demise of life. Any true happiness is life-supporting.

The classic form of primitivism is socialistic. It denounces civilisation on the grounds that it strips human beings of equality, freedom, and community. As they see it, civilisation is a killer of natural tendencies toward sensuality, communal sharing, peacefulness, playfulness, and reverence for nature. While many primitivists accept that we are now trapped in civilisation, they see many ways that we can improve physical, mental, and environmental health by following the example of our hunter-gatherer ancestors.

It is easy to dismiss primitivist viewpoints when one hears talk of anarchy and a retreat from civilisation as we know it. Yet primitivism is primarily a response to the monumental crises facing humanity. As such, it is worthwhile to study their criticisms of modern culture, as well as some of the solutions they offer. There is undoubtedly some merit in the primitivist argument that a quality heart-felt happiness is not possible once people have become insane in terms of their own natures, and their attitudes toward the planet upon which they and future generations rely for survival.

In his essay 'Feral', Zerzan describes the complete reversal in our understanding of the Palaeolithic world and pays tribute to it by saying 'Prior to agriculture, humanity existed in a state of grace, ease, and communion with nature that we can barely comprehend today.' By comparison, he adds, we moderns live in 'an upside-down landscape wherein real life is steadily being drained out by debased work, the hollow cycle of consumerism and the emptiness of high-tech dependency'.

As challenging as life may have been back then, it was aligned to our neurological and physiological heritage. Bjørn Grinde's book *Darwinian Happiness* develops this point as he speaks of the close match between the biological makeup and the living conditions of pre-modern people. According to Grinde, a good match between biology and the environment minimises stress and maximises the prospects for reward and gratification. While our potential for happiness expresses itself quite naturally under 'match' conditions, the main damper on happiness comes from what he calls 'discords'.

The concept of 'Environment of Evolutionary Adaptation' (EEA) is sometimes used to describe the conditions to which our genetics have become adapted. It is usually agreed that the human EEA reflects an environment that existed during the Middle or Late Palaeolithic period, from around 200,000 years ago until the dawn of agriculture somewhere between 15,000 and 10,000 years ago. A discord simply refers to a situation or set of demands that force people outside of their EEA.

While all discords do not necessarily have a negative emotional impact, there are many serious rifts between our biological design and the modern environment that diminish happiness. We dwell in what Grinde terms a 'Discord Society'. Its design slots people into situations that trigger low-mood brain circuits and gives rise to sweeping epidemics of depression, anxiety, and free-floating worry. He describes us as 'Stone Agers in the fast lane' who would be much happier if we could resolve some of the many discords that plague us. As Grinde sees it, one of the biggest discords preventing a genuine Darwinian happiness is the way in which moderns grow up without adequate parenting, sufficient nurturance, or social connectedness. These factors and others take a heavy toll on our sense of control, the ability to withstand adversity, and the quality of our relationships. Our immune system also takes a beating under extreme discord conditions.

Others have also argued that happiness is not easy today because we are not living like human beings. In his *American Psychologist* essay 'The Evolution of Happiness', psychologist David Buss describes the many mismatches between modern living and the type of life to which we were biologically programmed as animals. He too offers hope in saying that an understanding of these mismatches can be used to consciously readjust our lifestyles, preferences, and goals in order to achieve a more natural form of happiness. For instance, Buss lists some key ways that we can close the gap between modern and pre-modern conditions, thereby enhancing happiness and reducing the likelihood of depression.

Without claiming that we could or should live exactly like Stone Agers, Buss says that we can imitate our early ancestral world by increasing the closeness of our extended kin. This pertains to both physical and emotional closeness. Also, we could develop true friendships of the type that existed in an age prior to the 'fair-weather' friendships that dominate today. Another way of reconnecting to a native happiness is to begin once again to notice the gifts of nature that are sources of beauty, wonder, and nourishment.

The concept of an intact 'moral net' is sometimes used to express a situation in which people are experiencing maximum social and emotional well-being as a result of living in accord with their basic human nature. As Raoul Naroll wrote in his book *The Moral Order*, the 'moral net' does not refer to isolated individuals who are able to achieve well-being by meeting their own personal needs. Instead it refers to the overall fitness of a culture in terms of the intactness of its belief systems, social institutions, codes of ethics and behaviour, ritual and ceremonial traditions, initiation practices that establish a person's place within the group, and systems of activity that promote cooperation and harmony.

The word 'moral' is used in the broadest sense of the word. It is a measure of a culture's ability to meet indispensable needs such as belongingness, transcendence, identity, recognition, intellectual stimulation, and physical expression. A 'moral net' provides a framework that gives people a sense of meaning and purpose. It lays an existential foundation that lets people make sense of birth and death, and everything in between.

The 'moral net' plays an all-important role in creating the conditions for human happiness. A vast amount of anthropological research over the years shows that a weakening of the overall 'moral net' is the primary factor determining the prevalence of problems such as depression, anxiety, drug and alcohol abuse, marital breakdown, psychosomatic disorders, sleep disturbances, and delinquency. The general thrust of the data reveals that modernisation has the consequence of cutting away at the 'moral net' and making people vulnerable at all levels. All things considered, modernity seems to be rather backwards when it comes to emotional health.

Logic would tell us that a culture with an intact 'moral net' offers its members considerable advantages in terms of happiness. But testing this out has become very difficult because nearly all intact small-scale societies of the world have been largely destroyed by contact with the West. One has to go to the remotest parts of the globe to find societies that are still intact. Since some of these groups live somewhat similarly to their ancestors of thousands of years ago, they stand to teach us a great deal about the history of happiness.

In 1977, I spent a month at two remote Iban longhouses in the upper reaches of Borneo's Rejang River. This was shortly before the tragic cultural collapse that took place with the arrival of greedy American and Japanese logging companies, as well as the influx of 'cultural tourism' with their tacky 'Visit The Headhunters of Borneo' tours. Even so, some of their traditional ways had already been diluted as a result of some Western contact, as well as by the missionaries that had chiselled away at their belief systems, values, and traditional dress. There was also the growing trend for some young adults to leave the longhouse for employment and education. A small percentage returned and brought their newly acquired modern attitudes and paraphernalia with them. I recall one young man who had come back after two years in Singapore. He stood out in his 'Coca-Cola' T-shirt and had a forlorn look as if he were trapped uncomfortably between two opposed worlds.

Despite this, I came away with an unmistakable impression that they were a much happier people than those from where I had come. The Ibans were strikingly more tranquil and carefree. They smiled more, noticed more of what was around them, and approached each day with an untroubled ease that I had never before witnessed. To the extent that they offered a glimpse into the lives of people in pre-modern times, I had no problem believing that most of them were better off emotionally than the nail-biting folks in the fast lane of modern life. Their lives were undoubtedly more in accordance with the design of our species.

The anthropological literature contains quite a bit about the Ibans. The first medical anthropologists to encounter them were unable to find any evidence of 'neurotic' mental disorders. The longhouse is often described as an ideal type of social structure that is exceptionally well suited to the way in which we human beings evolved. For thousands of years, it provided a largely seamless cultural existence that gave people of all ages a clearly defined role, and a shared system of belief, ritual, and custom. It was the ultimate in terms of an intact, interconnected community. It left no cracks through which people could fall into the meaninglessness, alienation, and existential fog that plagues modern society.

Actually, what I found most remarkable about the Ibans was their sense of play. It showed through in subtle as well as obvious ways in nearly everything they did. What really hit me was that play did not seem to dissipate with age. I recall one day sitting at the river by the dugout canoes, watching the people and reflecting on the actual nature of play and what made it possible, as well as what extinguishes it. Play comes so naturally to us as children when it is the cornerstone of happiness. For children, play and happiness are synonymous. Unless they are socialised to override this instinct, they will crave play more than anything else. It is a universal phenomenon.

Happiness Key

Man is most nearly himself when he achieves the seriousness of a child at play.

– HERACLITUS

The Greek philosopher Heraclitus was not alone in believing that human beings are most in accord with themselves, and probably at their happiest, when engaged in play. Plato believed that a person's relationship to play was especially revealing: 'You can discover more about a person in an hour of play than a year of conversation.' Writer and philosopher G. K. Chesterton was even willing to say that 'The true object of all human life is play.'

In his remarkable book *Homo Ludens*, Johan Huizinga developed an entire theory about the evolution of human culture that revolved around our play instinct. At its most primitive level, it discharges super-abundant energy, and meets what Huizinga calls our instinctive 'need for relaxation'. Play also exercises our 'imitative instinct' and trains the creature to exercise restraint and judgement. It is a creative process and a means by which people express themselves socially and stretch their imaginations in a mutually enjoyable way. Play tests people's freedom and opens up new ways of looking at the world and its potential. It has a positive irrationality about it that lets us transcend literal formulas for cause and effect.

As Huizinga writes, 'Play only becomes possible, thinkable and understandable when an influx of mind breaks down the absolute determinism of the cosmos.' In this respect, one could describe play as one of the most sophisticated forms of intelligence.

To rediscover play is to rediscover ourselves and our full capacity for happiness. One could even call play a form of enlightenment that gives birth to the loftiest potentials within ourselves. To let playfulness slip away is one of the biggest blows to our prospects for happiness. Rather than set out to achieve happiness, many of us would do better by relearning how to make life into a form of play.

Play adorns life and gives it vital interludes that contribute to well-being. It represents an important life function, not only for the individual, but also for the effective operation of society as a whole. As Huizinga sees it, human culture crystallised on the play instinct, which provided a system to enable humans to create order from the rules that are inherent to the play process. The additional benefit of play as a basis for social organisation is that play tends toward the beautiful and the aesthetic, while fostering rhythm, harmony, and what Huizinga calls the 'noble traits' that encourage social interest. Of course, one does not need to take play quite so far in order to see it as an important contributor to happiness.

Writing when he did in the late 1930s, Huizinga had already noticed that play as a source of individual and collective well-being was vanishing quickly. It was being smothered by a new and more severe cultural system whose hub was work. Play itself was becoming like work, and was increasingly being absorbed into a business mentality. Complexity and constant change destroy the sense of play very quickly.

Since play is typically a social act that is pleasing in part because it is shared, it survives longer in societies that do not pit people against each other in lifestyles that revolve around competition and one-upmanship. In modern consumer culture, play is becoming more isolated, less physical, increasingly passive, and computerised. Social play is quickly turning into self-play that lacks wider value.

Even if their closer ties to their play instinct did not make pre-modern people happier per se, it certainly gave them a vehicle by which to express their exuberance for life. The topic of exuberance is not discussed much any longer simply because we do not see much of it in Western societies. Happiness itself has been drained of exuberance, which is why the happiness of today can appear pale and dispassionate, and why it can be so difficult to even tell who is genuinely happy and who is not. Exuberance was almost certainly a prominent part of the emotional worlds of pre-civilised people who had little if any reason to suppress their natural effervescence. Play is the main outlet for an overflow of passion for life. An absence of play usually mirrors a loss of this primitive passion for life.

CHAPTER FOUR

Prehistoric Happiness

PREHISTORIC people had no choice except to be swept along in union with themselves and the world. Life was in motion. There would have been no reason to step aside from the stream of life and speculate about how happy or unhappy they might be. When we conclude that life is bad or that it could be better, we are comparing our lives to another standard or type of life. The modern person is exposed constantly to alternatives that could easily make their own quality of life appear low by contrast. But the prehistoric person was not confronted with a long menu of alternate life possibilities.

Individuals were fully integrated into the group, as well as impregnated by the natural and spiritual worlds. There was no room for the type of happiness anxiety that provokes judgements about the value of one's private emotional portfolio. Individualism and narcissism were still a long way off. It is ludicrous to imagine that early hunter-gatherers put a primary emphasis on personal happiness. This only happens when the issue of happiness becomes a problem and when it is eyed from the sidelines of life. There was no need to make an effort to be happy. They had not yet been expelled from the natural order of things.

Modern people who feel that they are not sufficiently in touch with happiness are often out of touch with their emotions generally. By contrast, Palaeolithic people had a much higher degree of emotional intelligence of the type that lets one recognise feelings as they occur, identify the emotions of others, and act on emotions as they arise. These are things at which Palaeolithic people excelled due to their bond to the moment as well as an absence of abstract language that creates emotional static and doubt about one's feelings. Likewise, guilt and shame, both learned emotions that were unnecessary prior to civilisation, did not yet exist as constant temptations to muzzle genuine emotion. Palaeolithic people knew what they were feeling. They had not been sold on emotional fraudulence as a form of currency.

Certainly the more immediate experience of emotion in prehistoric times resulted in tensions that needed to be resolved as they arose. It had not yet become profitable to suspend, delay, or completely avoid conflict by sugar-glazing the emotions and working them like a business operation. A modern outsider looking in on their world might come away feeling that Stone Agers were not always being as nice as they could be. Yet the relative absence of emotional dishonesty bore fruits in terms of their ability to experience happiness and avoid the build-up of toxic emotion. This meant that they probably had ongoing means of catharsis, which refers to a beneficial discharge of emotion.

If the emotions were more alive in pre-civilised times, the same was probably true of the mind. Unlike the media depictions, they were not the blank-looking dullards that wallowed around in an under-stimulating environment. In his book *The Rapture of Maturity*, Charles Hayes writes that the primitive intellect was almost certainly much more active than what we find in the anti-intellectual modern age. Our immense inheritance of technology and information can create the illusion that we are mental giants by comparison to early people. But Hayes makes the case that, from that standpoint of the rapture that a well-exercised mind can deliver, the primitive environment was far superior to that of consumer culture with its steady diet of intellectual shortcuts and brain-numbing distractions. It offered more ongoing challenges and was a richer foundation for curiosity, exploration, and wonder. Few things are more closely associated with happiness than these. The native landscape was a perpetual classroom that not only edified but also fostered a genuine maturity. Hayes makes the following comparison between our early ancestors and the modern person whose mind has ceased to be a source of happiness.

> In primitive societies, all members who reached maturity were expected to use their intelligence in order to contribute to the good of the whole. Imagine the improbability of finding members of a hunter-gatherer society who expressed pride in their lack of knowledge about hunting and food preparation. Contemporary anti-intellectualism is no less ridiculous; we've just learned to accept it as normal. Among our Stone Age ancestors, survival depended upon devoting one's full attention to one's present activities, whatever they were at the moment. That we assume that our ancient ancestors were stupid reflects an enormous gap in what we refer to today as intelligence.

Happiness, however we end up defining it, always seems to hide in small and passing things. Conversely, the spectacular has always been a surprising flop when it comes to happiness. Without trying to romanticise prehistoric life, the people back then undoubtedly had a tremendous eye for detail. This was born from their here-and-now time location, and their need to be intimately attuned to the immediate environment. It had the effect of tuning them to all potential channels of happiness.

Happiness Key

It is the sides of the mountain which sustain life, not the top.

– ROBERT PIRSIG

These words are from Robert Pirsig's *Zen and the Art of Motorcycle Maintenance*. They are part of the following passage that captures the wisdom of living in the moment, which is the core of the Zen concept of mindfulness, the form of consciousness that is believed to be the source of all happiness.

Mountains should be climbed with as little effort as possible and without desire. The reality of your own nature should determine the speed. If you become restless, speed up. If you become winded, slow down. You climb the mountain in an equilibrium between restlessness and exhaustion. Then, when you're no longer thinking ahead, each footstep isn't just a means to an end but a unique event in itself. This leaf has jagged edges. This rock looks loose. From this place the snow is less visible, even though closer. These are things you should notice anyway. To live only for some future goal is shallow. It's the sides of the mountain which sustain life, not the top. Here's where things grow.

Mindfulness has been defined as 'paying attention in a particular way, on purpose, in the present moment'. It means 'on purpose' in the sense that the mind is focused and not distracted by competing thoughts and sensations. All this takes place in the Now, without contamination from future anticipations. When people are mindful, they can stay with an experience, and not have it be discoloured by negative emotions that intrude from other sources. This creates an emotional anchor that allows for feelings of calmness, contentment, and freedom. Our early ancestors had a high degree of mindfulness that led them to live on the sides of the mountain.

Happiness Key
Remember that happiness is a way of travel –
not a destination.
– Roy M. Goodman

It is still possible to see remnants of the type of mindfulness in which happiness is part of the journey, rather than a destination that never arrives. For example, around twenty years ago I had the honour of being escorted through the bush of Framlingham Aboriginal Reserve in Australia. My guide was the respected elder of that group of Gunditjmara Aborigines, an unforgettable man by the name of Banjo Clarke, nicknamed The Rainbow Man. Two things left an indelible mark on me, and both were reminiscent of a much different time, space, and consciousness than my own.

One was Banjo's astonishing ability to pick up on the subtlest of things around him. As we walked, he would point out birds and animals, sounds, colours, textures, and movements that eluded me completely. Banjo did his best to help me experience the majesty of the bush, but my senses were dead. He was operating at a level of perception far beyond my own. I was too far ahead of myself to be alive to what was around me. It was more than the fact that he was intimately acquainted with the bush, while I was not.

The second lasting impression I had was the profound connection that Banjo had with the bush, and with nature. He walked through it with reverence, and seemed rewarded by love and calmness. Banjo had an intense spirituality about him that radiated the long-lost knowledge of the sacredness of the natural order, and of our duty to respectfully concede to its genius. In the tradition of Aboriginal culture, one can never own the land, or any aspect of nature.

Before Banjo's death, Camilla Chance interviewed him on a number of occasions as part of the book she published about him titled *Wisdom Man*. When asked about his educational background, he said: 'I never went to school. The bush was my school. Plus our church, our spiritual world. Old people guided me all through this life.' Of the ultimate importance of the bush, as well as its power to deliver happiness, Banjo said:

> We just love peace and tranquillity in the bush. You got a sense of security because you got your ancestors' spirits there, guarding you against all evils. When you feel real good, you come back home, you forget all your troubles and you're right again. And when you're down in the dumps, you go back in the bush again and all them spiritual things come back to you again.

Australian Aboriginal culture is the longest continuous one in the world, extending back over 60,000 years. For this reason, the remnants of traditional Aboriginal culture that survived the European colonisation are often seen as the best window into the mind and emotions of ancient people. John Koch's book *Portal to the Dreamtime* uses a wide variety of ethnological accounts and first-hand conversations with Aborigines to revisit the 'archaic consciousness' that characterised a great many ancient hunter-gatherer societies. It is a type of consciousness that fostered a view of human life with sacred nature at its centre. This helped to safeguard the environment and to minimise blatant acts of irresponsibility toward the natural world. Also, its blend of mysticism, family and community focus, and initiation practices were all infused with the type of spirit energy that was a potent source of metaphysical happiness for early people.

The Aborigines expressed their highly spiritual natures through the complex cultural system known as Dreamtime. This is essentially their understanding of the world and its creation, and their way of bringing ancestral energy into the moment. It contains the great stories that explain the laws of existence. Dreamtime embodies the Aboriginal view that all life, both human and animal, coexists in an intricate unchanging relationship that is orchestrated by the spirit ancestors. It is a cultural belief system, with a rich set of rituals, which unites the physical and sacred worlds.

The reminiscences that Koch obtained from a number of Aboriginal elders express the high degree of positive emotion that flowed from Dreamtime energy. One recalled the collective mood that surrounded Dreaming ceremonies:

> Much joy here, much happiness here. Aboriginals – this place here was very happy for them, they were very happy here, and joyful. Much trouble later when white man came, but before that this was place of much joy. Great happiness for Aboriginal people here. Much to celebrate.

Another excerpt of the conversation refers to the abundant happiness that flowed from the timelessness of Aboriginal life:

> Here is happy, where we came to sit and greet our brothers and sisters in Dreamtime, and live in Dreamtime. You do not understand – your time is not the same time as our time. There was no time for Aboriginals. You have day and week and month. There are no days, weeks and months for Aboriginal people. We lived in eternal time. The full moon was our time. The seasons come and went, and my father got old and died, and my son grew up. But there was no time like your time. Happy time here, this place here was happy time. We had so much happiness here till the white man come.

The first Europeans to reach Australia could not help being struck by the happiness of the local inhabitants. The following description from the journal of explorer Captain James Cook, written in 1770, sheds light on the type of happiness that can unfold in a cultural climate of nature, spirituality, and simplicity.

> They appear to be in reality far more happier than we Europeans; being wholly unacquainted not only with the superfluous but the necessary conveniences so much sought after in Europe, they are happy in not knowing the use of them. They live in tranquillity which is not disturbed by the inequality of condition; the Earth and sea of their own accord furnishes them with all things necessary for life, they covet not magnificent houses, household-stuff etc., they live in a warm and fine climate and enjoy a very wholesome air, so that they have very little need of clothing . . . In short they seem'd to set no value upon anything we gave them . . .

A somewhat similar account of pre-modern happiness can be seen in the journal of explorer Thomas Jeffries as he first encountered the native people of California. His use of the phrase 'truly philosophical' is quite interesting as he tries to convey their exceptional degree of happiness.

> As they covet only the necessaries of life, with which nature has abundantly provided them, they scarce so much as think of its superfluities . . . the Indians are the happiest of all mortals . . . they neither know, nor desire to know, those false enjoyments which we purchase with so much pains, and with the loss of that which is solid and real. And their most admirable quality is that truly philosophical way of thinking, which makes them condemn all the parades of wealth and magnificence.

Influential British poet John Dryden, in his 1669 book *The Conquest of Granada*, was the first person to use the term 'noble savage':

> I am as free as Nature first made man,
> Ere the base laws of servitude began,
> When wild in woods the noble savage ran.

In 1663, in *To My Honour'd Friend Dr. Charleton*, Dryden hailed the Native Americans discovered by Columbus:

> The fevrish aire fann'd by a cooling breez,
> The fruitful Vales set round with Shady Trees;
> And guiltless Men, who danc'd away their Time,
> Fresh as their Groves and Happy as their Clime.

It was not only the European discoverers who pondered the apparent happiness of the natives. There are several early accounts of the natives themselves who were baffled by the obvious unhappiness of the European arrivals. They did not dance, sing, or celebrate. They laughed very little unless intoxicated. They had no magic. No miracles. The Australian Aborigines, who lacked any signs of pathological anxiety when they were first encountered, were struck by the perpetual agitation of the Europeans, and their dumbness about the happiness contained in nature.

Some Native American groups even began praying for the Europeans, which did not impress the conquerors who assumed a great superiority over the savages. The following 'Prayer for The White Man' invoked the ancestral Grandfather in hopes of reviving the spirits of the lost and destructive souls in their midst:

> And now, Grandfather, I ask you to bless the White Man. He needs your Wisdom, your guidance. You see he only feels comfortable when given power. Bless them, show them the peace we understand, teach them humility. For I fear they will someday destroy themselves and their children, As they have done so Mother Earth. I plead, I cry. After all, They are my Brothers.

There is currently a world-wide cult that has built up around the North American native peoples. One can find shops in Australia, Europe, and Asia that sell First Nations head-dresses, beads, weavings, and clothing, as well as literature about their wisdom and traditional lifestyles. First Nations cultures have come to represent a way out of the death throes of modern consumer culture. Many people who strive to achieve First Nations consciousness are convinced that it offers much more hope for human happiness and for a planet that we are not ashamed to leave our children.

In our age of political correctness, it makes us nervous to

even hint about social differences between people. We have also become paranoid of making generalisations, even if they stand to increase our understanding of an issue. For these and other reasons, many people have been reluctant to speak of 'happy societies' that once existed, or that might even exist today in places that operate differently than our own. Yet some people insist that there was indeed a Golden Age when spirits were able to soar higher than today. Descriptions of initial encounters with societies that functioned in a similar manner to our Palaeolithic ancestors almost always allude to the simplicity of life as a possible explanation for their greater happiness.

This comes through quite clearly in the sixteenth-century writings of Michel Eyquem de Montaigne. For instance, in his famous essay 'Of Cannibals', published in 1580, he speaks of the peaceable equality, and luxurious amounts of leisure, of the 'savages', adding: 'They are moreover happy in this, that they only covet so much as their natural necessities require: all beyond that is superfluous to them ... They have no lack of anything necessary, nor yet lack of that great thing, the knowledge of how to be happy in the enjoyment of their condition and to be content with it.'

In his 1744 work *The Enthusiast: or, The Lover of Nature*, poet Joseph Warton added to the chorus of voices proclaiming the happiness of 'primitive' people:

> Happy the first of Men, ere yet confin'd
> To smoaky Cities; who in sheltering Groves,
> Warm Caves, and deep-sunk Vallies liv'd and lov'd,
> By Cares unwounded.

Around this same time, Jean-Jacques Rousseau was lighting a bonfire under the 'happy savage' and anti-civilisation movements. His work is sometimes seen as the beginning of the modern study of cross-cultural mental health since he drew attention to societies that, unlike his own, appeared to be virtually free of psychological disturbance. He described entire societies that, in his words, were 'without hardly any disorders save wounds and old age'. By comparison, Rousseau writes in his classic 1754 work *Discourse on the Inequality of Men* that modern living, with its abundance of philosophy, civilisation, and humanity, yields nothing but 'a frivolous and deceitful appearance, honour without virtue, reason without wisdom, and pleasure without happiness'. He felt that civilised society leads people inevitably to adopt hypocrisy and dishonesty in order to feed their selfish interests.

By the middle of the nineteenth century, we seem to have had enough talk of the emotional supremacy of the happy and noble savage. Somehow this did not fit with the view we wanted of ourselves and the world. Some of this backlash was voiced by Charles Dickens in his witty 1853 article 'The Noble Savage' published in *Household Words* magazine. He defended civilisation, while cursing the 'howling, whistling, clucking, stamping, jumping, tearing savage' as a diabolical, amoral, and swinish creature that should be 'civilised off the face of the earth'. What seemed to set off this tirade was the publication of a book by traveller and artist George Catlin, describing the happiness, symmetry, grace, and perfect physiques of the native Ojibbeway and Loway people of North America.

If pre-civilised people were happier than those today, it was largely because they were more alive. In fact, the clamour for happiness that we see today can be understood as a metaphor for the modern struggle against feelings of deadness. Poet

Rainer Maria Rilke was alluding to this phenomenon when he wrote 'most people die of unlived life'.

As the anti-civilisation movement waned, fewer and fewer Westernised people were willing to accept that the life of the 'savage' was what the good Lord ever had in mind for us. The Victorian era encouraged emotional inhibition, while intensifying criticisms about the over-liveliness of the savage, all of which seemed depraved and dangerous. In truth, the 'savages' lived with a much higher degree of spirituality, into which clear moral codes could be woven, than people of the Victorian age or the contemporary age.

The gathering momentum of science and technology also helped to turn the evidence about happy 'savages' into a myth. The time was right for another sort of myth that saw 'progress' as a new form of this-world salvation. The growing belief that the good life lies in forward motion and advancement was incompatible with anti-civilisation models, and soon indigenous peoples became once again nothing more than 'backward'.

It did not help that some of the original accounts of native people painted them in an exaggerated way as beings of the highest virtue, without any corruption, malice, or selfish traits. When this turned out to be less than completely accurate, some people began to doubt the accuracy of the uncivilised happiness that was described by so many early anthropologists and explorers.

Yet, as we have also come to realise more recently, there was considerable truth to the claim that pre-civilised people were more peaceful and humane than their civilised counterparts. This runs counter to the stereotype of primitive people as violent and always eager to club each other on the head at the slightest provocation. But anthropological and fossil evidence shows quite clearly that societies that went the route of domestication were in fact the ones that became subject to violent practices. Despite some exceptions, organised violence was almost non-existent among non-agricultural groups.

It even turns out that many groups that earned reputations as fierce warrior societies were in actuality very peaceful until rising populations and food competition forced them to restructure themselves. For instance, there is little convincing evidence of organised violence among the New Zealand Maori population prior to the extinction of the moa, a huge bird that was the main food source of these early people, around AD 1500. It was not until the Late Palaeolithic era that territoriality became much of an issue for human beings. Prior to that, there were few of the types of inhumanity that stemmed from rival groups pitted against one another for control of resources.

Modern-day primitivists who are reviving the case for the happy savage sometimes credit the greater happiness of pre-modern people to their depth of spiritual awareness, or what is now being called 'spiritual intelligence'. This was bound up in their veneration of the natural world. Nature is the richest source of happiness for the human being. Thus it is not surprising that nature is often profoundly sacred in happy societies.

Gratitude is a distinctive trait in a high proportion of societies that are fused with the natural world, and that have a resulting reverence for nature. The Kung people of Botswana, for example, have an ancient tradition of giving formal thanks, and apologising, to any animal that they kill. Many pre-modern societies had a large number of thanksgiving ceremonies that took place at regular intervals. Their world did not have the type of safety nets and surpluses that led them to take for granted the bestowals of nature.

Happiness Key

Appreciation can make a day,
even change a life.

– MARGARET COUSINS

As American writer Margaret Cousins writes, there is great power in the ability to appreciate. It is the backbone of happiness. Many of the major philosophies and religions of the world have preached that happiness, truth, and beauty lie within the ability to treasure the small everyday gifts that we receive. It would have been almost impossible not to feel a deep appreciation for the life-giving fruits of the natural world, especially when it was so closely connected to day-to-day survival.

There is a calmness and serene joy that accompanies gratitude. When one is filled with gratitude, life becomes a sort of prayer. In the thirteenth century, Christian mystic Meister Eckhart spoke of gratitude in a way that helps us understand a road to happiness that was much more travelled in ages past: 'If the only prayer you ever say in your life is thank you, it will be enough.' Some recent research has confirmed the value of gratitude as a happiness aid. It was found that gratitude exercises, such as keeping a 'gratitude journal', could increase a person's level of enjoyment and overall sense of life purpose. Gratitude also fortifies spiritual meaning and directs people toward ways of living that are morally gratifying.

In their book *Spiritual Intelligence*, Oxford academic Danah Zohar and psychiatrist Ian Mitchell describe spiritual intelligence as the ultimate form of illumination where one creates the foundation for emotional well-being. It does not necessarily have anything to do with religion, although it can be expressed that way. Instead, it is a skill that involves creativity, awareness, imagination, and flexibility of perception. This is what enables the person to comprehend the wholeness of life.

But most societies have seen a gradual stunting of spiritual intelligence over the ages, and in particular in modern times. We now find ourselves victims of a 'spiritually dumb culture', as Zohar and Mitchell label it, that interferes with the ability to experience the world in a unified fashion. The happiest societies are often the ones with the greatest value placed on spiritual intelligence. This prevents divisions between the person, Earth, and the Unknown. It is this type of cultural arrangement that best resists restlessness, as well as confusion about one's place in the world. A deficit of spiritual intelligence underlies the perpetual yearning that bedevils the modern age. Impaired spiritual intelligence is one reason for the ongoing decline of compassion, which includes our growing detachment from nature.

The young field of cognitive archaeology is shedding additional light on the spiritual and emotional worlds of our prehistoric ancestors. Some fresh insights have come from new methods of interpreting ancient cave art. Researchers at the Rock Art Institute of South Africa's Witwatersrand University have led the way in this regard. Among them is David Lewis-Williams whose book *Mind in the Cave* helped to decode the meaning of cave art.

The trail of images that tended to lead from the cave entrance into the dark and nearly inaccessible inner recesses acted as a membrane between the everyday world and the sacred realm. Our direct ancestors, the Cro-Magnon people, tapped intricate mental networks that allowed them to harness altered states of consciousness in order to penetrate into the spirit world and participate actively in it. Such practices were already established around 30,000 years ago. According to Lewis-Williams, hallucinations, hypnogogic dreaming, and deep trance were the mental vortex associated with entry into the heart of the cave. A variety of methods were probably used to induce transcendent states and visionary experiences that transported the person into states of ecstasy and oceanic bliss. People had by then discovered that entry into these peak emotional experiences could be aided by fasting, rhythmic movement, repetitive sound such as drumming, or the ingestion of hallucinogenic plants.

The intensity of participation at sacred sites was probably such that the person could actually 'see' and interact with the spirits to whom the caves and its artwork were intended to give access. The spiritual initiation process was so persuasive that the initiate literally imprinted upon his or her unique guardian spirit. The spirit became a permanent part of the person. The relationship between the individual and this spirit developed further over the years and became a potent source of comfort, guidance, security, and confidence. It was an intimate connection between the human and spirit worlds that created a valuable foundation for the person's general well-being and happiness.

It is likely that assisted hallucinations played a key role in providing a spiritually based happiness, as well as other forms of positive emotion. The whole subject of hallucination has been turned on its head in recent years. Only twenty years ago, the word 'hallucination' was understood only in a strictly pathological way. To see, hear, experience, and communicate with non-existent forces invited a diagnosis of schizophrenia or a similar psychotic disorder. But in actuality, psychiatric types of hallucination probably represent a dysfunction of the normal brain functions that allow for high levels of imagination, creative dissociation, and sensory super-awareness, all of which are potentials inherent to our original design.

Research shows that, even today in the absence of cultural assistance, around 40 per cent of people report some sort of hallucinatory experience. In the past, hallucinations were an important vehicle by which to express the transcendent needs that are common to all human beings. Among other things, the direct contact that pre-modern people had with the spiritual world gave them a convincing sense that they were not alone. They had immediate sources of power to which they could turn. Rather than being the source of fear, hallucinations played a central role in their happiness and sense of life meaning.

Seeing makes believing very easy. The spiritual world of Palaeolithic people was so real and alive that they operated as true believers. They did not feel the sense of abandonment that underlies our collective cry for help. As such, they needed no coddling beyond what the spirits and their local group had to offer. Today there are almost no true believers of the type that inhabited the Palaeolithic landscape. The faith that is so crucial to happiness is almost dead.

Spirituality was a total way of life in pre-modern times, which leads us to ask about the relative advantages and disadvantages of religion from a happiness standpoint. If one looks at the full range of modern research on the psychological consequences of religion, such as that summarised in my previous book *Religion and Mental Health* as well as others on this subject, it is clear that the overall emotional impact on people is a moderately positive one.

This effect should be expected in light of the universal

nature of religious motivation. Very rarely does one find a universal evolutionary feature that does not operate on behalf of the human being. In fact, religion is so basic to the human being that a number of anthropologists have coined the term *homo religiosus* to describe the essence of our nature. By living so much closer to this aspect of their being, Stone Agers probably had greater spiritual or transcendent happiness. While their lives ebbed and flowed more with the chaos of earthly existence, heaven was not the waiting game that it has become today.

Human beings are happier when they have an ample amount of convincing magic in their lives. The word 'magic' can be used broadly enough to encompass all methods of blending reality and unreality in creative ways that foster a sense of control, meaning, and power. Magical thinking and magical experience are common to all cultures. They are inherent to humanity and play a valuable role in promoting the welfare of individuals and societies. In fact, it is hard to imagine any deep sense of happiness that does not have threads of magic woven into it. This is despite the endless criticisms that have been levelled against magical belief and practice, including religion. A completely stark and unfiltered view of existence would cause us to become capsized by too much reality.

Humans have the mental infrastructure to use magic to their benefit, even if fear is part of the price. Our early ancestors had a world that was full of magic. Yet magic is exceedingly difficult in the Age of Reason, which means that we may have lost something that has long helped to promote happiness. Increasingly, magic is being siphoned off by the emotionally parched world of materialism. Shopping malls are being built to resemble cathedrals. Products are being given religious-sounding names, and are advertised as being good for the soul. But consumption – even when it becomes sacred – turns out to be nothing more than a continuous feeding tube for distraction. The myth of luxury hastens the slide into emptiness.

We are creatures who crave the higher ecstatic order that magic is so capable of delivering. Entertainer Bette Midler actually did a nice job of voicing this craving in a semi-humorous comment she once made about her search for this lost realm: 'My whole life had been spent waiting for an epiphany, a manifestation of God's presence, the kind of transcendent, magical experience that lets you see your place in the big picture. And that's what I had with my first compost heap.'

The Palaeolithic mind was largely an unconscious one, as was the type of happiness it delivered. The self was almost entirely social and spiritual in nature. Conceptual consciousness had not yet developed to any great extent. Concepts such as ownership, profit, winning, losing, and success did not demand their attention and energies. But the advent of civilisation would change all this, as well as the way in which we would experience happiness.

CHAPTER FIVE
The Fall

SOME historians have written that The Fall, which refers to humanity's proverbial fall from grace, innocence, and happiness, can be understood as a fall into time. It was then that we became isolated from the stream of life. The concept of time is one of the great historical killers of happiness. Early in the Palaeolithic era, time did not exist beyond one's interaction with the natural world. There were no hints of the perpetual time crunch in which over-stressed moderns find themselves.

Before time was promoted to a primary guiding force, people's lives had a distinct orientation in the present. With little more than the sun as a rough guide to phases of day and season, this timeless fabric enabled spontaneous engagement with the moment. It enhanced sensation and fostered a crisp awareness of the immediate surroundings. Very importantly, it allowed people to fully experience a wide range of emotions, including happiness.

The pioneering French anthropologist Claude Levi-Strauss once wrote that 'the characteristic feature of the savage mind is its timelessness'. As he saw it, such an orientation was one reason that primitive people possessed 'a kind of wisdom practised spontaneously and the rejection of which, by the modern world, is the real madness'. The strongly futuristic bent of modern consciousness helps to navigate an unnatural world of constant man-made change. But anxiety would become part of the madness that future dwellers would have to bear.

Research has found that people living in future-oriented cultures have higher average stress and anxiety levels than in cultures that are more present-oriented. This is because living in the moment offers greater predictability and control, as well as more certainty about one's own experiences. On the other hand, the future is always a gamble. Its unpredictability locks future-oriented people into a state of tension as they blow in the winds of uncertainty and far-flung hopes.

While we usually think of Stone Age life as a daily hair-raising jaunt into an unknown world, the opposite is more likely to be the case. People back then knew exceptionally well what to expect from their world, and how to operate in it. Their minds were not taxed by a backdrop of constant change that forced them to get ahead of themselves. All-pervasive anxiety is the main byproduct of the futuristic modern age. So here again is an area where early people had an edge in terms of happiness. The arrival of futuristic consciousness would also open the door to another nemesis of the modern mind, namely worry.

Worry was a foul pill that had to be swallowed as we rejected the moment in favour of what might be, could be, or should be. Since worry is dependent on future focus and anticipation, which Stone Agers did not have to any great extent, there were probably very few worry-warts among them. By contrast, the chronic worry that afflicts modern people is reflected by the all-too-familiar symptoms of fatigue, agitation, irritability, sleep disorders, and muscular tension.

One might think that technological advancement would be erasing some of the worries that plague moderns. But on the contrary, we are somehow finding more and more things to worry about. The moment seems to be getting further away. The future grows more frightening. Michel Eyquem de Montaigne once said on the topic of worry: 'My life has been filled with terrible misfortune, most of which never happened.' Worry takes a serious toll on happiness. Being placed mostly in the here-and-now probably meant that Stone Agers did not suffer many misfortunes that did not exist.

It was not until around 5500 years ago that the concept of being 'on time' originated. This is when the first sundial clock made its debut, which allowed the day to be broken down into separate time units. The water clock, known as a clepsydra, appeared in Egypt around 3400 years ago, and was later used extensively in Greece. Much later, in fifteenth-century Europe, we would see the first mechanical clocks using a mainspring and balance wheel, another step toward a world that would eventually be defined by efficiency.

As the concept of time evolved and came to be measured more precisely, the past and future began to dilute the immediacy of experience, and to block access to our emotions. This also carried many advantages that translated into 'progress' and enhanced survival. But happiness became a more slippery quarry as time grew in status to that of a ruthless dictator.

It has also been said that The Fall was a fall into language. Palaeolithic people did not come to perceive themselves as happy or unhappy by way of a conscious appraisal that revolved around words. This undoubtedly boosted their capacity for happiness since happiness does not survive long in the intellectual domain. The use of language has a way of sucking the lifeblood out of happiness and destroying its authenticity. As German philosopher Friedrich Nietzsche said, 'words dilute and brutalise; words depersonalise; words make the uncommon common'.

Exactly when language emerged is still a matter of debate. But it is unlikely that language was developed to any extent during the Early and Middle Palaeolithic periods. The absence of formal language is one of several reasons that our prospects for true happiness are sometimes seen to be at their peak during the early stage of our humanity. Language is crude and almost always has the effect of distorting true meanings. In his essay 'Language: Origin and Meaning', John Zerzan writes that language limits one's attention to what is contained in the language itself, causing us to be cut off from our own experience and the rest of the world. He sees the proliferation of language as a main cause of our 'emotionally maimed modern life'.

To attach a word to the experience of happiness is to attempt an unnatural control over it. One quickly gets bogged down in the nearly impossible task of actually capturing happiness with words. While civilisation would be impossible without words, some have referred to the 'disease of language' that contains the seeds of sadness due to the way in which it often prevents us from going beyond words to where a more genuine experience resides. Language is also the mother of organised inequality. It is the main means by which people create categories and separate themselves into conflicting groups. Without formal language, the Palaeolithic world offered limited opportunities for people to rank themselves in terms of others, which is a common cause of unhappiness and rage today.

Language emerged, not so much for additional mastery of nature, but for political reasons. It provided the methods of coercion that would enable a minority to manipulate the energies of the majority. Language expanded for the suppression of emotions, which made it easier to herd people into roles that ran counter to their animal inclinations. For the first time, language made possible deceits that helped to remove people from their own emotions, and to confuse them about what made them happy. The use of language to befuddle people about their own experience has triumphed in the double-speak and spin-doctoring that can be heard at every turn of modern life. Thus our chances for happiness may have taken a blow with the advent of language and lies, even though these were crucial springboards for what we think of as civilisation.

One aspect of the historical isolation from happiness and other forms of experience is the way in which language transforms the active into the passive.

Happiness Key

To happiness the same applies as to truth; one does not have it, but is in it.

– THEODOR ADORNO

Happiness operates like truth, as twentieth-century German philosopher Theodor Adorno tells us. It is not a fixed state at which one can arrive with suitable gimmicks. One has to be in the river of life, and in the process of living. But Adorno felt that staying in it has become almost impossible today. As such, he was rather pessimistic about our chances of happiness since the modern age interferes with 'the unrestricted openness to experience' that is so vital to self-discovery. In describing how people become closed off to experience as they conform to the rigours of consumer capitalism, Adorno writes 'Happiness is obsolete: uneconomic.' Despite all the things that made life precarious and brief, Palaeolithic people were in it. Almost nothing could be taken for granted. Life had not yet become a matter of economics.

The legacy of a world that offered lots of movement can be seen in the earliest forms of language, which were made up of nearly 50 per cent verbs. Early languages had a myriad of words for things that could be seen, touched, and smelled, which reflected the sensual quality of life. They contained a great range of terms and phrases to describe various types of actions. As civilisation gradually transformed the active into the passive, the percentage of verbs continued to decline. The English language currently contains less than 10 per cent verbs, one of many reminders about the passive creatures we have become. Somehow, happiness must now find its way into the hearts of people who spend much of their time sitting, staring, and passively indicating their choices. We have become a shopper in the broadest sense of the word.

Looking again at Palaeolithic cave art, we get another reminder of a former world that was alive, interactive, and in motion. The artwork incorporated rituals that allowed active communication between the human, spiritual, and natural worlds. The people themselves were not the main subjects of the art because they were part of a much bigger story that was being told. As civilisation encroached, the artwork becomes steadily more stiff and indicative of a world that was increasingly bridled and bureaucratic.

To say that prehistoric people were active agents who were necessarily part of the natural cycle of life does not mean that they were physically on the move all the time. In fact, it is widely accepted that they had an abundant amount of leisure time. Stone Agers probably mixed short working days with extended periods of lazing about, resting, and playing.

In looking at more contemporary groups of hunter-gatherers, such as the Kung people of Botswana, one sees that they hunt for only around six hours per week. Research with the San bush people of South Africa showed that they worked the equivalent of a twenty-hour week. They spent vastly more time than modern people engaged in socialising, exchanging ideas, philosophising, and developing artistic skills. When not doing these things, they were free to dabble, sleep, or partake in anything that pleased them.

Even laziness, which has an undeservedly bad reputation, serves an important role in happiness and health. All top predators have evolved tendencies to laze about for periods of time. This is especially true of big-brained creatures such as human beings. Big brains crave idleness just as much as they do stimulation. If they do not get it, they begin to function like small brains.

Wedding oneself to ceaseless work is not a sign of intelligence. It can even thwart the creative workings of the unconscious, which thrives on idleness. Many of the world's greatest discoveries and insights were born from indolence and unstructured musings. Einstein, a devoted daydreamer, once said that the happiest thought of his life came to him while languishing in a daydream. This thought, in which he pondered the feeling of weightlessness that would be experienced if someone were to leap off a roof, eventually led to his theory of general relativity. By contrast, hitching one's wagon to workaholism destroys the freedom that is so necessary to happiness.

The ability to take emotional advantage of freedom and free time has been largely lost. But things were much different in pre-modern times. In his 1932 essay 'In Praise of Idleness', Bertrand Russell points out that our early ancestors had not yet been indoctrinated into believing that everything needed to be done for the sake of something else. Unlike today, he says, 'There was formerly a capacity for light-heartedness and play which has been to some extent inhibited by the cult of efficiency.'

For the sake of human happiness, Russell recommended that working hours be reduced to no more than four hours per day. In today's work-fixated society, this would cause many people to panic since their lives have become one-dimensional except for brief breaks from work. But the fact that modern people would not know what to do with free time is not a statement about human nature. Instead, it is an indictment of modern life and the way in which it funnels far too much human energy into work, leaving people at a loss to convert their freedom into happiness. What we have come to think of as 'down time' is pregnant with possibilities for high-quality happiness, something that was well known to people of former ages.

Between 15,000 and 10,000 years ago, a monumental trans-formation occurred in human populations around the globe. This was the shift from hunter-gathering to agriculture. The word 'agriculture' does not carry many negative connotations for us today. But it was a pivotal development that a number of historians equate with The Fall. Some have described the arrival of agriculture as the beginning of our descent into captivity. It brought with it many problems that would spell an end to the type of happiness that existed when we lived more in harmony with our human nature. This is why primitivists see agriculture as our point of departure from a truer form of happiness, and into an inferior 'tamed' or 'trained' form of happiness. It was the advent of agriculture that forced us to live outside the environment to which we had been adapted for countless millennia.

Happiness Key

But what is happiness except the simple harmony between a man and the life he leads.

– ALBERT CAMUS

Existentialist Albert Camus gets to the heart of happiness when he equates it with harmony of living. To be in harmony with one's nature and the life one is living is also to be happy. Domestication and its repressions jolted the person out of harmony with nature, oneself, and others. Among other things, it blinded us to our animal natures and our location in the bigger scheme of life.

There is no doubt that the shift toward a primarily agricultural existence took a major toll on people's physical well-being. Fossil evidence shows clearly that early farmers, by contrast to their hunter-gatherer forerunners, had a significant loss of stature, more bone disorders, a reduced life span, increased infant mortality, a higher rate of infectious and chronic degenerative diseases, more dental problems, and far more nutritional deficiencies. Prior to agriculture, there was no tuberculosis, malaria, cholera, smallpox, measles, or plague. Cancer was almost non-existent in Palaeolithic times.

On the subject of cancer, Russian oncologist Mikhail

Sivashinskiy leads the way in demonstrating that modernisation is the underlying cause of cancer. In arriving at his overall conclusion that 'Modernity is cancer-prone', he points out that the toxins that make modernity into a lethal carcinogen are not only physical, but emotional, social, and spiritual as well. In his recent conference paper 'Capitalism and Cancer', he argues that the immune system of people living in modern culture is weakened by their proneness toward artificiality and pretence, repression of feelings, inhibition of creativity, stress, frustration, loss of family, existential emptiness, the absence of permanence, a loss of control, and a largely fragmented existence. Despite its obvious advantages, he sees the current system of addictive consumerism as one of the worst arrangements for general health and happiness. It conceals many psychological poisons that rear their heads in ways we are yet to fully understand.

In their book *African Exodus*, Chris Stringer and Robin McKie summarise the dire consequences of the dawn of agriculture:

> Healthy hunter-gatherers with excellent physiques were suddenly turned into sickly hunched over farmers. Although it is often promoted as the great technological achievement that freed men and women from the drudgery of hunting and gathering food, farming took a grim toll of its practitioners.

In fact, it was only around 100 years ago that mechanised farming, technology, and medical advances began to reduce some of the damage wreaked by agricultural living.

The physical ill-effects of agricultural living, which brought with them many emotional costs, were due to a few main factors. One was the change from a richly varied diet to one that revolved primarily around a single food source, such as wheat, rice, and maize (corn). Stringer and McKie give examples of some Native American groups who, around 1000 years ago, shifted from a hunter-gatherer existence to a farming one that was centred on corn. After a detailed analysis of skeletons found in the burial mounds of Ohio and Illinois, they conclude: 'Far from being one of the blessings of the New World, corn was a public health disaster.' They reached a similar conclusion with regard to the early farmers who lived from 11,500 to 7500 years ago at Abu Hureyra, in Syria, who came to rely on a similarly narrow agricultural existence.

The health problems that arose when hunter-gathering was abandoned were not merely the result of dietary factors. Being an agriculturalist involved lots of hard and repetitive work. Men laboured arduously with the cultivation, while women had their bodies punished by long hours of grain preparation, usually by kneeling at saddle querns on which they rolled heavy stones to crush the grain. Analysis of bone from the early days of farming showed that a high percentage of adults, and even many children, suffered from painful deformities and osteoarthritis of the hips, lower back, knees, and toes. Crushed vertebrae and damaged discs were common. Life for so many of the ancient tillers was quite literally a pain in the back. Chronic pain has always been a major block to happiness and peace of mind. The consensus among historians is that the move from hunter-gathering to agriculture was not by choice. People saddled themselves with ploughshare and harness, and bore all the physical and emotional disasters, out of necessity. Colin Tudge writes about this in his book *Neanderthals, Bandits, and Farmers*:

> The Neolithic people did not embark on a life of arable farming because they wanted to, or because they saw the advantages of cereals. They did it because they were forced into it when their

paradise was taken from them and they were shoved together
into hills that just turned out to be especially hospitable.

Much of the Old Testament is about arable farming, even
though it was written several thousand years after the original
farmers. Of this, Tudge writes: 'The Old Testament can in
fact be read like a bumper edition of *The Farmer's Weekly*,
and the stories it tells are horrendous: of famines, of slave
labour, of unremitting toil.' It is not the story of a happy
people. Yet, agriculture was a solution of sorts once human
numbers reached a point that made it impossible for everyone
to survive off the natural environment. A plot of land had
almost unlimited potential as a food source.

It was at this stage that the idea of 'work' was born; that
is, spending one's energies in an otherwise unpleasant and
unnatural way out of necessity. Also awakened in us was an
association that would stalk us from that point on, namely that
the more one worked the more one was able to support. With
fertility and reproduction as crucial motivations of that age, the
first 'benefit' for the budding 'working being' was to be able
to support more children. The more work, the more children.
But this also meant the more children, the more work, which
is why the transition from hunter-gathering to farming was
the original baby boom, even though it was a terrible bust
for health and well-being. A vicious cycle took over that saw
a parallel rise in population and work. More mouths to feed,
but more work to keep them fed.

Agriculture planted in people's minds the seeds for overkills
of all sorts. These lurked in the perception that we are not
constrained by nature. All it took was work to transform
nature from our parent into our slave. But thinly disguised

in this new form of hope was our own slavery. Before that, nature did most of the work. Agriculture signalled the arrival of a type of slave success that would put us on an unceasing treadmill and prevent a return to Eden. There would simply be too many people to turn back. As time went on, the bane of overwork and overpopulation would continue to negate the benefits of slave success. It would be the largest single hurdle to human happiness.

Shortly after the global switch to agriculture the concept of happiness was born. It followed on the heels of a sense of loss as we entered a realm that was alien to the blueprint of human nature. To this day, the quest for happiness can be traced to an archetypal nostalgia for what it was like to be fully human and fully alive.

A residual sense of displacement became part of our collective unconscious. It can be seen in every generation of civilised people. The vast majority, both past and present, feel that the world is sick. When surveyed, around two-thirds of people will agree with statements to the effect that 'the world is falling apart', or 'society is collapsing'. Even the 'happiest' and most optimistic of people usually confess to feeling that the world has gone stark raving mad. This feeling has intensified in recent times due to rapid cultural disintegration. But it is an ancient phenomenon dating back to The Fall.

Tales and stories about Eden emerged not long after the advent of agriculture. This reflected a type of existential homesickness. But we would never again find our way home, emotionally. As newly domesticated creatures who were chained to back-breaking labour, the Golden Age was still fresh in the minds of early farmers, and the time was ripe for myth-making. Eden itself is the voice of folk memory about the happiness and ease of life that existed in the easier hunter-gatherer age.

Some historians have been quite specific about the date and location of the biblical Eden. They say that it was a region of the Persian Gulf that, 10,000 years ago, was a wonderfully fruitful plain, criss-crossed by several rivers. At that time, life in this area and a few other parts of Western Asia seemed to have been especially idyllic. The hunter-gatherers had acquired by then enough knowledge about horticulture to partake in the simplest of sowing techniques. Basically this involved gathering the seedpods from especially desirable plants, sprinkling the seeds about, and letting nature do its thing. This made it even easier to reap the food sources that would supplement the meat from their hunts. The hunts themselves were not demanding due to bountiful game.

Thanks to a combination of several favourable factors, life may have never been easier, or more relaxed. Skeletal evidence from the region confirms a relatively stress-free existence. There were hardly any indications of trauma as evidenced by violent injuries, healed fractures, debilitating diseases, or nutritional problems. There were very few signs of hypoplasia, a thinning and grooving of the tooth enamel that archaeologists often use as a measure of emotional and physical stress. These are among the reasons why historians of Eden sometimes see this period in the Persian region of the Middle East, just prior to the yoke of full agricultural dependence, as the paradise that legend would recall.

But the fact is that stories about a former Golden Age, when we were the happy children of nature, cropped up in agrarian societies all over the globe. A great many of them have persisted to this day. Aside from those, virtually all societies since the birth of agriculture have been marked by a 'good old days' mentality. Some of the earliest recorded writings allude to better days in the past, just as contemporary people pine over the happier, simpler, and easier life of former generations. But no generation was probably much happier than any other once we left behind the Golden Age and crossed the threshold of the golden cage, from which there was no escape.

As this cage got smaller, we would come to display more and more of the behaviour of big predators that are forced into captivity: depression, rage, social withdrawal, perversion, and agitation. We found ourselves in an overcrowded zoo that was highly noxious for emotional and mental health. This would be a cultural zoo in which we would flourish in proportion to our mastery of nature.

CHAPTER SIX

The Golden Cage

CIVILISED culture grew more complex in order to accommodate the large and growing numbers of domesticated humans. It allowed for the labour requirements of society to be divided up. Rules were introduced to decide who were the masters, scullions, winners, and losers. To maintain control, people's energies were standardised by inventing rules to govern all aspects of life, consciousness, belief, and action. It was all very different to the social structure of pre-civilised people, who lived in small groups that functioned more along the lines of large extended families, or small self-reliant communities. Even though civilisation was a physical coming-together, it amounted to a drastic break from the wholeness of the pre-civilised world. It involved people becoming slotted into narrowly defined roles, and being separated from one another by the power and status that differentiated these roles.

The actual word 'civilisation' derives from the Latin *civis* that translates into 'citizen' or 'townsman'. The following is a typical definition of this enterprise: 'A civilisation is a complex society in which many of the people live in cities and use agriculture, as distinguished from band and tribal societies in which people live in small settlements or nomadic groups and make their subsistence by foraging, hunting, or working small horticultural gardens.'

If one accepts that we do in fact possess a nature that is more aligned to a hunter-gathering mode of existence, it is not difficult to imagine that civilised cultures can tarnish emotions through frustration, disharmony, and discontent. One strength of Sigmund Freud's theory of human behaviour was his ability to see the conflict between civilisation and human nature. This is why he writes in his 1930 book *Civilization and Its Discontents* (originally titled *Unhappiness in Culture*) about the impossibility of such a thing as civilised happiness. With the shift from natural to domesticated living came repression, which was always at odds with happiness.

Civilisation and repression are so closely linked that it is not possible to understand one without the other. Eventually we would become civilised out of our natural state to such a degree that we would no longer be certain of our identity as a species. An awareness of this led Ralph Waldo Emerson to warn 'The end of the human race will be that it will eventually die of civilization.' Short of that, there is probably a point at which becoming over-civilised begins to deplete happiness. This explains why those in the anti-civilisation movement feel that true happiness can only be found by opposing the colossus of repression that we know and celebrate as civilisation.

The loss suffered in the course of becoming a civilised toiler is conveyed in many notions of Utopia that appeared over the ages. In story form, these go back to the earliest days of civilised life. Some of the oldest Greek writings are about the lost Utopia where humans were happier and freer. In the seventh century BC, Hesiod grieves in *Works and Days* about a former Golden Age when people 'lived as they were gods, their hearts free from sorrow and without hard work or pain; when the fruitful earth yielded its abundant harvest to them of its own accord, and they lived in ease and peace upon the lands with many good things'.

Virgil's *Eclogues*, written between 42 and 37 BC, recalls a vanished Utopian era of peace and abundance, in which people's modest needs were provided for by nature, without the need for wretched toil. A glowing account of the lost Utopia is given by Roman poet Ovid in Book One of *Metamorphoses*:

> Golden was the first age, which, with no one to compel, without a law, of its own will, kept faith and did the right. There was no need at all of armed men, for nations, secure from war's alarms, passed the years in gentle ease. The earth herself, without compulsion, untouched by hoe or ploughshare, of her gave all things needful.

There was no way for the many utopians throughout the ages to actually know the exact nature of pre-civilised life. But as with stories about Eden, each one probably contained some amount of inherited memory about happier times. The happy Land of Cokaygne, about which the early Greeks romanticised, was a utopian vision about a former paradise where idleness and freedom reigned supreme. Most of the early utopian reminiscences were about a time when drudgery was unnecessary, and when people's inclinations were not held hostage by alien laws. The last lines of the fourteenth-century English poem *The Land of Cokaygne* read: 'Every man may drink his fill and needn't sweat to pay the bill.' All civilisations hark back to a time when their hands were free of thick calluses, and their hearts free of worry.

Blood, sweat, and tears would be a bigger part of the picture for human beings as they crowded against one another, and became exposed to new forms of social control. The natural autonomy of former times would give way to the might of centralised authority. As people became further domesticated, the vast majority of them would end up as part of a herd that was shepherded by a new and largely unseen force, namely politics.

Happiness and politics never went together very well. A political animal lives in the smallest of cages and shows many symptoms of solitary confinement. When viewed in light of human nature and its needs, outside political control is highly unnatural. From day one, positions of political leadership would act as a magnet for the insane. But politics was inevitable once we fell out of nature. All sorts of issues would arise concerning land rights, ownership, sharing, and power relations. People's lives needed to be dictated like never before. The girdle of political authority steadily tightened to the extent that external controls over people were almost absolute. Slavery became possible not only in the figurative sense, but in the literal one as well.

In ancient Egyptian civilisation, approximately 10 per cent of the population were actual slaves. This number increased considerably as Egyptian civilisation progressed and became more focused on foreign conquests, which added prisoners of war to the slave ranks. It is estimated that upwards of 30 per cent of people throughout the early Roman Empire were slaves. The percentage of people who are enslaved in the modern age would depend largely on one's definition of slavery. It would include almost everybody if we appreciate the concept of economic slavery.

In his eulogy of the 'happy savage', Rousseau wrote how they had 'no judgement on accomplishments' and, like a happy child, 'no awareness of capacity and desire, power and will, and artificial needs'. But all of these were about to change. Timelessness and living within the moment were not desirable attributes from the standpoint of domesticated mass culture. Neither was unrestrained sensuality, insatiable curiosity, or the passions generally. None of these were ideal traits for an animal that needed to be goaded efficiently. The ideal citizen was one who had a high tolerance for conformity, routine, and emotional suppression. Of course, all of this sounds quite modern, which is why it has been said that the history of human happiness was completed by 5000 BC. Not a great deal has changed since then in terms of our potential for happiness within the confines of tamed existence.

Just as the body was coming under added pressure from increasingly complex cultural demands, so too was the large spiritual component of human nature. Primitive spirituality was an invitation to chaos in the new order of things. Standardised ways of belief and practice were more conducive to herd control, even if that meant some loss of spiritual happiness. It did not take long for civilised culture to erase the former intimate spiritual bonds.

As happiness became more elusive under the strenuous and increasingly alienated conditions of civilised living, both the nature of happiness and the means to achieve it became shrouded in mystery, as it still is. Confusion reigned in early philosophies about happiness. The idea of harmony with nature as a primary foundation for happiness had become largely extinct by the time early Greek civilisation was reaching its peak.

Happiness Key

The goal of life is living in agreement with nature.

– Zeno of Elea

Zeno, the fifth-century BC Greek philosopher, was speaking of the high-quality happiness that comes by way of synchrony with the natural order. But his words are among the final whispers that would be heard in Western civilisation about this deep form of happiness. By 3000 BC, it had already become exceedingly difficult for people in large-scale Western civilised societies to experience nature with any degree of respect. Western civilisation had organised itself around the wholesale razing, manipulation, and exploitation of the natural world.

As the domination of nature became the equivalent of the destruction of nature, it was psychologically more convenient to view nature with indifference and even disdain. Western civilisation would manufacture a combination of economic and religious rationalisations that would justify a ruthless abuse of nature. This, along with our arrogance, would accelerate over time, and the abuse would even become a warped basis for happiness. By the time that materialism blossomed fully as a credible format for happiness, much of what would make people 'happy' would depend upon the death of nature.

The old adage *homo homini lupus* ('man is a wolf to man') gradually became a reality as civilisation and overpopulation continued to corrupt relationships with fellow human beings and nature. In response to this, many ancient philosophies of happiness revolved around a return to goodness, as well as overcoming our tendencies to do ill to others. This approach could not lead people back to a primordial happiness. But it made philosophical sense for them to foster the qualities of righteousness that could avoid the repercussions of the mounting conflict and wolfishness.

The idea of happiness as an extension of virtue can be found in the works of great ancient philosophers. But more than that, many of these philosophies were embedded in wisdom about the art of living. They often pointed the way to universal truths about happiness that went beyond the importance of moral intelligence. In the fifth century BC, Greek philosopher Democritus described the way in which happiness could not be separated from justice, decency, and gratitude: 'The cheerful man is strong and free from care, but him that cares not for justice and does not the things that are right finds all such things joyless. The right-minded man is he who is not grieved by what he has not, but enjoys what he has.'

A generation later, Plato carried on in this vein in saying that living justly was essential to happiness in this world. In its purest form, the type of morality-based happiness that he preached could actually run counter to the individual's own interests, which is not at all consistent with modern egocentric understandings of the happy life.

Happiness Key

A tear dries quickly when it is shed for the troubles of others.

– Marcus Tullius Cicero

Cicero viewed moral depravity as the primary evil that intercepted people from happiness. He even believed that exposure to suffering could help to stimulate the character development necessary for eventual happiness. For Cicero, happiness that comes by way of virtue bestows a strength that makes the person impervious to pain, and able to take bad fortune in their stride: 'No one can be happy except when good is secure and certain and lasting, for our wish is that the happy man be safe, impregnable, fenced, and fortified, and so made inaccessible not only to a little fear, but to any fear at all.' Like several other philosophers of his age, happiness was seen in part as something that had desirable defensive properties that could serve one well in a hostile world. But the type of happiness of which he spoke could also promote compassion and a willingness to sacrifice oneself for others, which he believed was good for the soul.

The ancient Cynics and Stoics viewed moral achievement as the single highest form of good, and thus the only true requirement for joyous living. Some of them went so far as arguing that happiness obtained through virtue would empower a person to remain happy even while undergoing torture. Aristotle rejected the notion that happiness could withstand even the agony of torture. Yet he stressed excellence of character, and regarded moral bliss to be the touchstone of true happiness.

Modern big business would have a collective seizure if classical Cynicism ever staged a return. Diogenes, a student of Antisthenes and founder of the Cynic school of thought, was said to have lived in a barrel with no possessions other than a bread bag, stick, and robe. This made it impossible for anyone to rob him of his happiness. Diogenes once said 'He who has the most is content with the least.' He and his Cynic followers would undoubtedly be the world's worst consumers.

Epicurus, the third-century BC philosopher and father of hedonism, taught that happiness resulted from the maximisation of pleasure and minimisation of pain. This could best be accomplished by remaining in the here-and-now: 'The man least dependent on the morrow goes to meet the morrow most cheerfully.' But Epicurus also believed that this hedonistic approach to life was the best means to judge what is beneficial to oneself and society. As part of this, Epicurus saw excessive desire as an unhealthy trait that blocked the path to happiness, tranquillity, and harmonious relations: 'There are times when we pass by pleasures if they are outweighed by the hardships that follow.'

Happiness Key

Nothing is enough for the man to whom enough
is too little.

– Epicurus

While Epicurus saw happiness in terms of positive citizenship and respect for community, he also realised that one can easily become a lackey to what he called the 'mob', as well as the rulers of the mob. For him, freedom from the influence of the masses was crucial to one's well-being. He was far ahead of his time in seeing a passion for possessions as a toxic trait that deprived one of freedom and the ability to live life pleasantly and wisely: 'A free life cannot acquire many possessions, because this is not easy to do without servility to mobs and monarchs.' How remarkably pertinent those words are today in light of people's servitude to their unrelenting material needs.

Zarathustra, the prophet of ancient Iran and the first great teacher to incorporate ethics into religion, equated happiness with goodness: 'Happiness to him who gives happiness to others.' His philosophies about ethics as well as happiness were summed up in his counsel 'good thought, good word, good deed'. Happiness had developed a new enemy in the form of evil. All over the civilised world, happiness prescriptions were bearing the signature of a world that had taken on a new dark side. It is no coincidence that variations on the theme of original sin began to appear in many ancient civilised cultures.

Some early Chinese philosophies realised the wisdom of letting go, even of the quest for happiness. Confucius reminded people in the sixth century BC that 'to be truly happy and contented, you must let go of what it means to be happy and content'. Lao Tzu, the sixth-century BC Chinese philosopher and founder of Taoism, says this very explicitly in *Tao Teh Ching*: 'One must renounce happiness in order to gain it.' He goes on to speak of the need to arrive at a state of absolute purity through a rejection of external desire:

> Always without desire we must be found,
> If its deep mystery we would sound;
> But if desire always within us be,
> Its outer fringe is all that we shall see.

Unlike Western philosophies, nature continued to hold an esteemed position in many Eastern doctrines of happiness. Classical Taoism taught that people must give up hope for things outside of themselves. In the third century BC, philosopher Chuang Tzu expressed the Taoist view that the human being and its activities are pathetically insignificant by contrast to the majesty of nature: 'A man in the universe is like a pebble or a twig in the mountains. As such he can only obey nature. He may be useful in a small way, but it is beyond him to originate anything.' To the Taoist, nature must be cherished, and never defied or defaced.

Taoism taught that a successful life requires one to forget

about everyday this-world matters, and even about the state of the human condition itself. To have Tao and happiness, one must give up words, knowledge, and facts. In so doing, one enters a joyous realm in which there is nothing to worry about, nothing to figure out, and nothing to wait for.

As a philosophy, Taoism is especially interesting since it is opposed to most aspects of civilisation. It stresses the importance to resist the endless seductions, distractions, and falsehoods that are spawned by political and social forces. Taoism teaches that societal norms should be avoided. The only laws that favour the good life are the laws of nature. Human laws are not only unnecessary, but they rob the person of the freedom required to live a 'native' life. Taoist philosophy was pessimistic in that it saw happiness as something over which the person had little control. It was the domain of rare individuals who were wise enough to understand that happiness comes only when one stops trying to improve things for oneself.

There is an inherent sadness to Taoist philosophy. Not many mortals can resist the urge to adopt societal norms. They cave in to the culture traps that drain the possibility of happiness. Some of this Taoist attitude is captured in the mournful Chinese saying 'On quiet nights, the elephant can be heard tugging at its chain.' We, the elephant, have surrendered our liberty and happiness in learning to perform for society. But no matter how good a performer we become, a life force within us tugs at those chains. However, most of us stop short of tugging hard enough to become free and happy. The cultural chains can feel quite soothing.

Early Buddhist philosophies revolved around 'Buddhi', which comes from the Sanskrit word meaning wisdom. It refers to the bliss that fills the self once enlightenment is achieved.

Similarly, Hinduism described a lofty state of being that could be developed through the stages of intelligence, bliss, and existence, in that order. Both traditions saw separateness as the worst form of heresy. The failure to curb selfishness was viewed as the principal destroyer of wisdom and happiness.

Buddhism, which was founded in Northern India by Buddha Gautama in the sixth century BC, is even more negative than Taoism when it comes to earthly happiness. As with Taoism, it rejected society. But Buddhism focused largely on the avoidance of suffering, rather than a self-centred quest for happiness. The self was seen as something that gravitates toward craving and illusion. Traditional Buddhism saw happiness as an inner peace that fills the space left by a reunification of the self. The ideal human condition was considered to be spiritual enlightenment that operated independently of social contaminants.

The highest level of consciousness, according to Buddhist philosophy, is one in which the person has given up everything, including the wilful rummaging for happiness. Kindness, tolerance, compassion, and reverence for life are thought to flow from this exalted realm. Buddhism is sometimes said to be the philosophy that is the least conducive to happiness. Yet Buddha himself held out a vision of a world where everything and everybody would be happy, as voiced in his following blessing:

> Let all beings be happy, weak or strong, up high, middle or lower state, small or great, visible or invisible, near or far away, alive or still to be born, may they all be entirely happy. Let nobody lie to anybody or despise any single being whatsoever. May nobody wish harm to any single creature out of anger or hatred. Let us cherish all creatures as a mother her only child.

May our loving thoughts fill the whole world, above, below, across, without limit, with a boundless good will toward the whole world, unrestricted, free of hatred and enmity.

Especially intriguing is the recent research showing that Buddhism-practising people have higher levels of happiness than their non-Buddhist counterparts. This has been explained in terms of the ability of Buddhist ritual to activate areas of the brain responsible for positive mood. Meditation enhances coping by allowing the person to better deal with emotions such as anger, fear, and anxiety. Buddhist practices seem to have an overall calming effect on the person. They can also unleash one from entrenched mental states like hatred, greed, and negative expressions of ego. Researcher Owen Flanagan of Duke University concludes: 'We can now hypothesise with some confidence that those apparently happy, calm Buddhist souls that one regularly comes across in places such as Dharamsala, India, really are happy.'

A number of excellent books have given detailed accounts of what the ancient philosophers had to say about happiness. But it would be a mistake to equate any one of these philosophies with the actual views about happiness that were held by ordinary citizens. Most of the philosophies of happiness referred to ideal states that were not reachable by many people. The early Greek philosophers, for example, spent a good deal of time trying to judge who in fact deserved to be called happy. The importance they attached to this matter implied that their awarding of happiness was reserved for a rather elite minority who somehow managed to meet all their criteria. It would have been a considerable honour to be deemed happy by them, and one not easily achieved.

The same is true for the lofty type of happiness that is set out by philosophers in addition to the Greeks. For instance, Chinese philosopher Confucius saw happiness as an offshoot of moral impeccability which he felt consisted of five qualities, namely 'gravity, generosity of soul, sincerity, earnestness, and kindness'. At the same time, he lamented the dire shortage of individuals who ever achieved this state of happy virtuousness: 'I have not seen a person who loved virtue, or one who hated what was not virtuous. He who loved virtue would esteem nothing above it.'

Happiness Key
Never value anything as profitable to thyself which needs walls or curtains.

– MARCUS AURELIUS

In his inspirational book *Meditations*, published in AD 167, Roman Caesar Marcus Aurelius was also preaching substance and virtue as the bridge to happiness. But crossing that bridge is again not easy. He warned that happiness will only come once we have purged ourselves of any values 'which shall compel thee to break thy promise, to lose thy self-respect, to hate any man, to curse, or to act the hypocrite'. Happiness is found in 'the mind of one who is chastened and purified, with no corrupt matter, nor impurity, nor any sore skinned over'. He contrasts this to the more common, but inferior, type of 'giddiness' that he said requires 'remedies'. If he were alive today, he would be dumbstruck by all the giddy types of happiness that scream out to be remedied.

In most cases, happiness was seen by the ancient philosophers as a sort of end state that mirrored a high degree of character development, life achievement, and fulfilment of aims. It was the culmination of a life lived to its perfection. Getting there was not nearly as important as finding the way to happiness. Even if one still had a long way to go, being committed to the difficult path was seen as victory enough. The happiness described was not the 'anything goes' type of mass happiness of modern times, which is sold as a quick and easy feat, and something that is the automatic birthright of everyone, regardless of one's merits or stage of moral and intellectual growth.

CHAPTER SEVEN

The New Trinity

LEAVING aside the philosophies of their day, happiness was viewed by the average person in pre-modern times as a manifestation of luck, and more specifically the outcome of divine favour. The world revolved around things far greater than solitary individuals. It was inseparable from the supernatural. Happiness was something for which one prayed or wished. *Eudaimonia*, the ancient Greek word for happiness, is an assembly of terms that quite literally means a 'good spirit' (or 'good god') who works on behalf of a person. The word *dysdaimon*, or unhappiness, translated into an evil spirit, or demon, that had come to bring misery and misfortune to someone.

Nearly all of the early civilisations had gods and goddesses of happiness to whom the average person could pray. For thousands of years, Hindus have prayed to Lakshmi, the goddess of happiness, harmony, and good fortune. Even today, millions of Hindus offer prayers to her, and adorn windows and doors with small lights that guide Lakshmi into their homes. Her 108 different names are chanted as part of the prayers to this cherished goddess. The Romans had the goddesses Fortuna and Felicitas, and the Celts had Gwen. Hetpet and Hathor were the Egyptian goddesses of happiness and joy respectively, while Xilion was the Aztec goddess of happiness. In ancient Tibet the goddess Dorje Naljorma was the bestower of happiness, while early Filipinos had Suklang-malayon.

The intimate association between happiness and luck can also be seen in the early English usage of the word 'happiness'. It originally appeared in English in 1340 and was spelled 'happinesse'. It derived from 'happ-chance', of Middle English and Old Norse origins. Today the word 'hapless' still means unlucky, whereas 'happenstance' and 'haphazard' imply a fate that is largely a result of chance or luck. The modern German word for happiness, namely 'gluck', is also the word for luck. Spanish, French, and Portuguese words for happiness also trace closely to words meaning luck, fate, and chance.

Happiness became more of an issue, and a source of hope, with the expanding perception that we were at the helm of our own lives. But well into the Middle Ages, people's expectations in terms of happiness remained modest. Human beings were still secondary instruments to much greater powers, and there was still a keen realisation of life's limitations. This was compounded by the prevailing Christian belief that happiness had to be postponed until the afterlife, when this veil of tears was finally lifted and we were rewarded by God with eternal bliss.

This view of supreme happiness as a feature of the afterlife has tempted some historians to say that medieval people had given up altogether on prospects for happiness in this life. The so-called Dark Ages conjures up images of a dismal emotional wasteland where gloomy people are merely waiting for God, while squandering their talents and potentials. Even God had become a rather dreary and demanding character who was exceedingly stingy with this-world offerings. In short, life did not seem to have much room for happiness, which explains the Christian adage 'Call no man happy until he is dead.'

It is true that medieval folk shared the belief that mortals were irreparably corrupted, and that sinful human nature was incapable of being perfected in an evil world. But in some ways they were probably advantaged by their deliverance from the whole issue of happiness, which usually has the paradoxical effect of promoting happiness. So maybe things were not quite as bleak as we sometimes think. Beyond that, they could supplement the tantalising promise of ultimate ecstasy in the afterlife with a preparatory state that came to be called grace.

The emotional fruits born from grace are touched upon by Puritan preacher Thomas Brooks who wrote in his 1657 book *Heaven on Earth*, 'The being in a state of Grace will yield both a Heaven here and Heaven hereafter, making a man's condition happy, safe, and sure.' Similarly, in *Institutes of Christian Religion*, Calvin portrayed grace as the great antidote to the squalor, suffering, and enslavement of earthly existence: 'When the favour of God breathes upon us, there is none of these things which may not turn out to our happiness.'

To be full of grace was to feel the type of joy that came from knowing one to be in a sufficient state of goodness to warrant eventual blissful union with the Creator. Grace was the bridge between the natural and supernatural worlds. It was a powerful instrument. People could act on it in the here and now. The accumulation of graces brings with it the feeling that one is progressing toward spiritual perfection and eternal happiness. In his chapter 'Heights of Happiness' from his classic book *A Companion to the Summa*, Walter Farrell wrote that grace itself was not a virtue, but rather a personal gift from God that became the foundation for supernatural values. It was the guideline by which the person judged merit, meaning, and purpose.

The actual pursuit of grace, Farrell added, took the person into the field of drama. The action of grace could be experienced as a soaring to divine heights, a justification for one's existence, an infusion of divine wisdom, and a peaceful reconciliation between God and one's imperfect self: 'It is the drama of sunrise conquering night, of escape from darkness and slavery into freedom and light, the drama of the prodigal son and his father's unquestioning pardon.'

Grace functioned in the same way as magic. The rituals that appeased God could also add assets to a spiritual bank account that could be cashed in on Judgement Day. Grace was a form of wealth. It conquered nature and made this-world existence a stepping-stone to future happiness. But it was also a vehicle for this-world happiness. As Farrell said, 'with grace there is no place for slavery, for irresponsibility, for brutish plunging into the sensible in an attempt to escape humanity. By grace man reaches his supreme dignity, and a full realisation of all that here and now gives a foretaste of that happiness which will be had fully when grace reaches its climax in glory.'

Enough grace could make people 'leap for joy' and be overcome with the Holy Spirit. In fact, the emotional worlds of people living in the Middle Ages were propped up considerably by the Holy Spirit, which had the power to instil an ecstasy far superior to anything contained in mundane this-world happiness. While not everyone took full advantage of this, many medieval people found relief from the slog of life by turning to the Holy Spirit, especially in times of hardship.

The Middle Ages gave birth to a great many 'Ecstatics'. The greatest examples of these were the medieval saints and their followers. Among them was Saint Francis of Assisi who experienced states of ecstasy so profound that he felt the forest to be on fire. His biographers describe a person who also had an enormous capacity for cheerfulness and spontaneous enjoyment in his everyday life.

Ecstasy is the highest form of temporary happiness. It is a deeply moving supersensual experience in which consciousness forges intimate unions with deeper elements of reality, culminating in what is sometimes called 'a single state of enormous intensity'. Ecstasy is a passionate, transcendent journey that transports the person to the One, the Absolute, and the 'great life of the All'.

Words usually fail to do justice to the experience of ecstasy. The most famous of the ancient Greek ecstatics was third-century BC philosopher Plotinus who was able to experience a 'contemplative rhapsody'. He described this as 'another mode of seeing, a simplification and abandonment of oneself, a desire of contact, rest, and a striving after union'.

In his book *Ecstasy*, Michael Eigen argues that the quest for ecstasy is a primal motivation for human beings and that it has been a sought-out experience for most of our history. He writes that 'the ecstasy of being alive is the core of our existence'. The sense of profound aliveness that lies at the heart of ecstasy was never too far away in primitive times. According to Eigen, it was a natural outcome of the contrasts and opposites – death and life, pain and pleasure, agony and elation, light and dark, male and female – that have always been the springboard for maximum aliveness. But today our encounters with natural types of ecstasy are rare without artificial chemical aids. The average person has lost touch almost entirely with this dynamic type of emotion that can enrich life, expand horizons, and rewrite one's perspectives and priorities.

Happiness Key

I know what the cure is: it is to give up, to relinquish, to surrender, so that our little hearts may beat in unison with the great heart of the world.

— Henry Miller

Ecstasy and other lost forms of peak emotional experience are dependent upon a 'letting go', and a merging of the self into a sphere of reality that is much bigger than the lone individual. The idea of surrender as any sort of answer or 'cure', as author Henry Miller termed it, has become foreign to modern people who have come to value personal power. But the act of surrendering opens up pathways to happiness that cannot be achieved in isolation. To surrender oneself is an act of strength that allows happiness to enter by way of the truth of our meagreness. It also opens a person to the higher grade of happiness that comes through the realisation of the oneness and interdependency of all life.

Religion is one of many contexts in which one can reap happiness by way of surrender. In his book *The Hebrew God*, German theologian Bernhard Lang uses the example of the ancient Israelites to illustrate how happiness is often amplified when the good life is understood as arising from forces greater than oneself. These people were unable to conceive of a good and happy life that was not mediated by God. They believed that God, or Yahweh, revealed himself as the agrarian deity The Lord of the Harvest, who granted all the gifts that sustain life. According to Lang, this offers a 'Third Function' of happiness that cannot be experienced in the absence of a bigger, and in this case a supernatural, mediator.

Lang emphasises the value of attributing life-giving gifts to a godly power, and sees this as a natural human tendency that facilitates happiness. He draws on biblical insights in illustrating how happiness does not reside in the actual availability of earthly gifts, but rather in the act of reflecting on them and interpreting their significance. This type of joy that the ancient Hebrews enjoyed is described by Lang as:

> an experience that is had when worldly goods such as food, children, and social and economic success are experienced as being granted by God. The fact that these goods are appreciated as coming from the hand of God and considered as signs of divine presence and friendship is of capital importance. It is apparently the act of associating the good life with God that transfigures life into something sacred and of ultimate value. The very act of associating God and the good life constitutes happiness. The loving presence of Yahweh frees human happiness from its radical limitations and gives it transcendent dimension, thereby completely transforming the structure of happiness.

Aside from religious surrender, there are many ways in which positive emotions can be magnified by interpreting them in a context that is much wider than ourselves. Love, life, and nature offer fertile possibilities for freeing ourselves from the illusion of our own significance, and for enriching it with a transcendent quality. Sometimes it is even possible to get a slight taste of ecstasy by simply lying on one's back on a dark still night, turning off all thought, and losing oneself entirely among the infinity of heavenly bodies. It is purely the result of surrendering oneself to the majesty of something that is immensely larger than ourselves. Our nothingness can be a great source of happiness.

As we continued to become our own deities, it was nearly impossible to see beyond ourselves. The notion of an afterlife began to seem irrelevant in light of the heaven that now began to seem possible in this life. Those who still clung to a belief in the afterlife responded by embellishing it greatly. Whereas the afterlife of the Middle Ages was a perfectly happy one, it was still a fairly sober religious affair that lacked many bells and whistles. But by the late seventeenth century, the Christian afterlife had become a sort of pleasure palace. This too was doomed by rapidly growing expectations of this-world happiness.

By the late eighteenth century, the promise of eternal happiness, as well as any happiness that could be extracted from the preparation process, was fading. It was being replaced by a more direct assault on happiness, which was rapidly relocating itself in this world.

Commenting on the message of American preachers, Alexis de Tocqueville wrote at the turn of the nineteenth century that one could no longer be sure 'whether the main object of religion is to procure eternal felicity in the next world or prosperity in this'. What he was observing were the beginnings of the type of religion in which God exists to serve us in this life, while we act as our own saviours. God was in active training to become the happiness coach for the human side.

The arrival of the Enlightenment saw happiness in the West become much more of an earthly affair, even for those who still considered themselves to be devout Christians. Interestingly, some of America's founding fathers were among the last great voices to speak of virtue as the best door to happiness. In

1776, the year of American Independence, Benjamin Franklin declared that 'virtue and happiness are mother and daughter'. Also in 1776, Thomas Jefferson, one of the authors of the Declaration of Independence, commented that 'happiness is the aim of life, but virtue is the foundation of happiness'.

The Declaration of Independence would itself enshrine people's inalienable right to the 'pursuit of happiness'. But this pursuit would soon depart from virtue. The father of happiness had already become the individual, who was on the way to becoming God. Happiness had become a virtue in itself. It would not be too long before unhappiness would be considered the worst of all possible sins. Happiness had finally wrested itself free from luck, fate, and God, even if this would result in a paperback version of happiness from that point on.

The eighteenth-century philosophy of John Locke foresaw the changes that were taking place in people's perception of happiness. He basically equated happiness with pleasure. More than that, he regarded pleasure as a virtue, and one that God was cheering us on to achieve. Christ, Locke argued, was a 'happy Christ' who was not beyond the pleasures of wine, dance, and banquets. This picture of Christ had considerable appeal in an age where people were beginning to see the light at the end of the dark tunnel of human existence. Arguments were being made that Christ may have actually been a happy-go-lucky guy after whom we might model ourselves.

Technological advances were freeing people from their hopelessness about happiness in this world. Products and services were beginning to appear that could lighten the burden of work, and create more time for this-world leisures and pleasures. But at first it was only the wealthy who could actively experiment with the new type of happiness that could be bought and sold. Until the middle of the twentieth century, the majority of people were still held captive by financial constraints and restricted opportunities.

With the 'death of God', the road was paved for a new trinity in the form of 'me, myself, and I'. There was a growing sense that happiness was a do-it-yourself job. In this atmosphere, the self-help book made its debut. The first one was titled *Self-Help: With Illustrations of Character and Conduct*, published by Samuel Smiles in 1859. The actual contents could not be more different than today's snap-your-fingers type of self-help books. Smiles's advice was still wrapped in old-style values, which led him to emphasise such things as thriftiness, fortitude, education, integrity, and social duty. In so doing, he was trying to keep alive the priority of moral character in the face of emerging free-market opportunities arising out of the Industrial Revolution.

In the decades that followed Smiles's book, economic trends continued to eat away at people's social and psychological supports. This amplified their collective sense of abandonment as well as the feeling that they needed help. Today, despite having tremendous amounts of advanced technological power at their disposal, moderns are shadowed by a sense that they need help, and lots of it. This is no longer limited to the 'developed' world. In India, for example, the demand for self-help and motivational products is increasing by 25 per cent each year. Happiness is becoming big business there, just as it has in the West. Anyone who can help is handsomely rewarded. No amount of information, advice, or self-help books can entirely ease this burden.

The rising numbers of psychologically orphaned people came to feel that they needed help with virtually everything

– how to meet people, how to make love, how to raise their children, and how to eat. Books cropped up on how to get angry, how to listen, how to discover erogenous zones, and how to say no. This underlying feeling of personal ignorance that afflicted moderns did nothing for their confidence, control, or security. Nor did it boost their general prospects for happiness. But it was reassuring to know that some sort of help was available.

By the time the cultural soil was prepared for the self-help industry, all coherent visions of happiness had faded. The seventeenth century saw the first inklings of happiness as a feel-good operation that people could perform on themselves. But it would take another couple of hundred years for community and religion to decline sufficiently for people to see themselves as free-floaters who needed to find happiness on the landscape of their own whims. There was no legitimate guidance from any source, which made them easy prey for the mushrooming ranks of helpers and emotional con artists.

The problem was that most of the helpers themselves were also thoroughly confused about happiness. As a result, the happiness help that began to flood in from many sources was loaded with contradictions and competing recommendations. To this day, one runs across how-to happiness books that offer ludicrous combinations of 'steps' toward happiness. Chapters on the need to go full-throttle toward personal achievement stand alongside ones on the importance of not taking oneself too seriously. Urgings on the importance of chasing your own private dreams are followed by ones on the ultimate value of family, friends, and community. Nothing should stop us from becoming financially successful, but we should realise that money does not make us happy.

The modern customer of happiness products has a bewildering mish-mash to untangle. Early on, self-help books tried to teach people that happiness and the good life could not be separated from healthy relationships and collegiality. But as time went on and people began to see themselves as islands adrift in a sea of alienation and indifference, the tone of the books became much more along the lines of 'do your own thing'. If you wanted to be happy, you just turn to yourself, your only true friend and the only one who really cares. It would lead to a lonely happiness, but happiness nonetheless.

Modern happiness was quickly becoming stripped of all substance, and slipping away from matters of the heart and soul. Self-satisfaction was being equated with happiness. Noticing this trend, John Stuart Mill scorned the new low-level happiness in his 1863 work *Utilitarianism*: 'Better to be a human being dissatisfied than a pig satisfied, better to be Socrates dissatisfied than a fool satisfied.'

Without social, spiritual, moral, and intellectual anchors, happiness was beginning to resemble a form of emotional masturbation. It could still feel good, but not like the real thing. All one needed was a basic knowledge of technique. Some purists would begin condemning this as a pseudo-happiness that lacked social value. But a massive market was opening up for anything that could bring on this self-service pig-satisfied version of happiness. The age of the individual was turning happiness into a solo act.

CHAPTER EIGHT

Happiness for Dummies

THE journey to a private, trivialised happiness was sped up by the arrival of positive thinking. Words had staged an assault on the emotions, and a thinking type of happiness was set to conquer. Norman Vincent Peale's 1952 blockbuster *The Power of Positive Thinking* sold over 20 million copies in forty-one languages. The age of self-talk had made its debut, and happiness was the first state into which we would try to talk ourselves.

The idea behind positive thinking, or positive self-talk, was simple. As Peale stated: 'Change your thoughts and you change your world. Our happiness depends on the habit of mind we cultivate. So practise happy thinking every day. Cultivate the merry heart, develop the happiness habit and life will become a continual feast.' It was a timely concept in an age where people were beginning to suffer so much psychological overload that they were eager for a happiness that did not tax the emotions, even if people only ended up *thinking* that they were happy. The growing queues of burned out and bedraggled people were reaching the stage at which they were happy to feel nothing.

But Peale's original positive-thinking model would soon be modified due to his demanding claim that the good life was dependent upon working to become a good, responsible, other-centred person: 'Never advance our interests at someone's disadvantage. We are to turn our back on evil, and in every way possible, do good, help people and bring blessings into their lives.' He preached the need to resolve unconscious emotional conflicts, whether by psychotherapy or faith. He even went on to blaspheme the god that had arisen in the form of ourselves: 'Nobody stands in control but God.' So it was not long before other panaceas arrived to train people to self-talk their way to happiness with less effort and more personal convenience.

The positive-thinking gurus never made it clear why or when people had actually embarked on the wretched course of negative thinking. It did not, and still does not, make sense that people will set about thinking negatively if the result is to get punished with unhappiness and other unsavoury emotions. Part of it may have been that, by the twentieth century, the world had become negative and ugly from a human standpoint. People's sense of safety had been compromised. Their belief in a better future was vanishing. Escapism became the main crutch. Anyone exercising any degree of realism could easily succumb to the 'negative view of the world' that is the main symptom of depression. Whatever the reasons, there was born a hearty appetite for a happiness that required no preparation, like the frozen TV dinner that, by the 1960s, was quickly replacing real food.

Not many people were pausing to ask about the merits of perpetually asking oneself 'Am I happy?' Yet a few social critics were saying that this is the world's dumbest question, since the continual appraisal of one's happiness is the surest way to extinguish it. In his 1954 book *The Passionate Mind*, Eric Hoffer went as far as to say that 'The search for happiness is one of the chief sources of unhappiness.' To appreciate this irony, we need to realise that happiness does not survive for long in the thin atmosphere of consciousness. More than that, it is never a good sign when a person, or a society, needs to drag up unconscious functions and manipulate them in the field of conscious thought. It means that it no longer comes naturally.

A number of other people were being turned off by the way in which happiness was dumbing people to matters of greater importance. The rapidly worsening state of earthly affairs led some of them to knock the blind march toward a happiness wonderland. They described the shameful legacy that we were leaving our children in the form of pollution, global warming, deforestation, overpopulation, development gone mad, the collapse of family and community, racial and religious conflict, terrorism, the widening gap between rich and poor, and so on. In *Homage to Clio*, W. H. Auden boasted 'I was glad I could be unhappy.' In making the point that the new personal happiness had become a form of neglect and ignorance, he used the analogy of a rooster who pronounces his happiness as all his sons are systematically castrated and eaten.

Happiness Key

To hell with it. Who never knew the price of happiness will not be happy.

– Yevgeny Yevtushenko

Russian poet Yevtushenko touches on a core truth about happiness in saying that it must have a price. But the late twentieth century saw a breed of people who hankered for happiness without a price, or at least one that could be absorbed without feeling the pain that gives birth to it. Happiness without a price made a mockery of the real thing. But it was the age of imitation, mimicry, and impressions. People had by now gotten used to a world in which nothing was real, and happiness did not need to be an exception in this regard. Happiness was destined to be a 'theme' in most people's life. People would embrace it as real enough, just as a theme park is a real enough experience for many.

The 1960s spelled a turning point wherein an entire generation woke up to the realisation that life did not need to have limits of any sorts. Suddenly, rules were out and feeling good was in. Happiness was now there for the taking, and without conditions or stipulations. A new radical hope had arrived. Happiness had become both free and available for the masses. Just a decade earlier, happiness was still being portrayed to some extent as a hill that needed to be climbed. This can be seen, for example, in Martin Gumpert's 1951 book *The Anatomy of Happiness*, which has painfully level-headed chapters on the importance of continual learning, accepting the reality of death, accepting one's limitations, working toward honesty, and paying for everything as you go along.

God, who for so long had kept a lid on ultimate happiness in this life, buckled almost completely in the 1960s and decided that he wanted everyone to be happy. Feel-good religions began to spring up under all sorts of names. Services gave way to polka music, electric guitars, big-screen projectors, pop-style vocalists, television cameras, celebrity guests, and motivational speaking. Attendance dropped sharply in churches still dealing in the bad news about life and ourselves, or in the need to sacrifice in order to know God. The business-style Christian mega church was born in which the preacher-cum-celebrity used charisma and media savvy to sell star-struck followers on psychotherapy-like prescriptions for this-world happiness and prosperity. It currently dominates the mass spirituality market despite increasing competition from motivational evangelists and psychological preachers whose infomercials and syndicated talk shows reach millions of potential converts to the power of ambition and the glory of psychobabble.

What came to be known as 'Positive Christianity' invited us to create our own destiny. It did not matter that the audience was filled with people who were often ignorant of basic religious doctrine. What was important was that religion had joined the feel-good revolution. In truth, that was the only thing that could have saved it from death in the emerging climate of entertainment and distraction. Today there is a popular belief that God's plan is for us to be happy. He does not even care if we get happy in ways that are diametrically opposed to the word of Christ. The triumph of the trivial was complete once God joined in and made happiness virtually unconditional.

The 1960s flower child motto 'live for the day' recalled the pre-civilised days when one basked in the type of joy that only exists in the moment, unblemished by past and future considerations. The older generation watched on in horror as the happy hippies, many of whose happiness had a chemical kicker, threatened to dismantle the foundations of civilisation itself. Young people were attacking everything that did not feel good, from war to brassieres. They just wanted to be happy. In their idealism, they did not see why the entire world could not be happy.

There have been attempts to frame the current happiness craze as a type of movement, along the lines of the hippie movement except that the soil for its germination was Los

Angeles rather than San Francisco. But this ignores the deeper social factors that have made happiness into such a fixation. Even so, it is true that many of our current happiness gurus were in fact former flower children. There is also an historical link between the hippie movement and the origins of the modern symbol of happiness, the happy face.

Mocked by some as the face of brain-dead optimism, the happy face was the brainchild of Harvey Ball, a graphic artist who became the promotions director of a company whose workforce was plagued with low morale. One day in 1963, to promote positive spirit, he drew the modern version of the happy face and distributed copies to all employees. He earned a measly forty-five dollars for that stroke of genius.

But it was two entrepreneurs from Philadelphia who eventually saw the real potential for turning the happy face into a money tree. They were in the business of marketing fad-items. In 1970, amidst the upheaval of the war in Vietnam and the open hatred of the younger generation, it occurred to them that the world was ready for a symbol that could replace the controversial peace symbol. They set about looking for one that had mass appeal and a pacifying effect on the anxiety-ridden public. Then one of them recalled seeing the original happy faces several years previously. The slogan 'Have a Happy Day' was added, and the rest is marketing history. Within two years, over 50 million smiley-face buttons had been sold. Today their numbers are out of control.

Nostalgia still surrounds the hippie movement. There are hippie specialty shops where one can buy all the gear and try to keep alive the dream. Websites have sprung up to do the same, such as www.happyhippie.com, which offers hippie paraphernalia of all sorts, as well as the Happy Hippie Forum to keep people posted about news and events. But the 'be here now' philosophy underlying the revolution was never going to last in a world giddy with progress and hell-bent on manufacturing a consumable happiness.

The 'Human Potential' movement took off in the 1960s. Largely counter-cultural in nature, it promised happiness by way of ongoing personal development, rather than passive cultural conformity. Among other things, it helped change the image of psychotherapy, which for the next couple of decades was used by many people as a growth experience that could enrich one's overall experience of life. Being honest, authentic, and real was seen as essential in order to come alive as a human being. Learning how to locate and express one's emotions was seen as a crucial step toward becoming a real person who could reach a genuine happiness. Discovering how to love in an honest way was part of this.

For a while in the 1970s, Arthur Janov's primal scream therapy even enjoyed considerable popularity. Janov's rationale was that 'everyone in this society is in a lot of pain'. He felt that screaming loud enough and long enough could replace pain with happiness, while also unlocking potential. Despite the obvious limitations of this approach, at least it addressed the need to give people some outlet for their negative emotion. Modern laughter therapy ends up serving some of the same therapeutic functions as past approaches such as primal scream therapy. The people promoting forced laughter are even claiming many of the same health benefits as the former promoters of primal screaming, namely reduced anxiety, stress relief, greater relaxation, and better sleep.

Humanist therapies were especially popular since they promised feel-good results. This was a welcome break from Freudian psychoanalysis that basically helped people adjust to their civilised unhappiness. In fact, there is a famous quote by Freud to the effect that 'I can help you transform your neurotic misery into common unhappiness.' That was no longer enough for modern people who increasingly were pinning their hopes on personal happiness.

What humanism and the Human Potential movement were offering made good sense in terms of happiness. That is, restore contact with others and oneself, and find one's way back to a more natural existence. But this was asking too much of a society of people who were spreading themselves very thinly and struggling to look after their minds, bodies, spirits, and even their children. Their values were proving to be completely at odds with those values that were supposed to lead to a humanistic happiness. It was an increasingly inhuman world in which fast-paced people were gearing their happiness efforts toward objects. But their limited energies were being drained from all directions as time grew shorter in supply. What they still itched for was a ready-mixed microwaveable happiness that did not require them to become something or to take their eye off the ball.

The 'New Age' movement helped a bit in this regard. It emerged as a branch of the waning Human Potential movement that could shorten the travel time to happiness by enlisting the spirit world. Despite its many faces, New Age happiness came down to finding the key to one's 'inner divinity'. Crystals, spirit guides, channellers, pyramid power, potions, auras, enchanted scents, and many other supernatural aids were introduced in order to both heal people and to whisk them toward the happy life. One major appeal of New Age happiness was that much of it could be had through the simple act of purchasing an object or service. This pushed happiness one step closer to the marketplace that it would later call home.

While New Age happiness continues to be popular today, it is limited by the fact that it requires people to believe in something outside of themselves. The things in which people need to believe are vague and often contradictory. This did not stop various New Age gurus from predicting the dawn of a global happy consciousness once a critical mass of positive energy could be achieved. But this dream faded as the consumer age accelerated the process of churning out depressed shoppers whose lives had been reduced to a series of rushed choices.

The year 1979 saw the coining of the term 'Age of Depression' to describe the general state of mind of Western people. Rates of depression and youth suicide were skyrocketing, the family was collapsing, religious coping mechanisms were vanishing, stress levels were shooting up along with materialism, and people were steadily increasing their working hours in the pursuit of the good life. Tuning out was in. A massive denial had set in regarding the dire state of the environment. The seeds of unhappiness had been sown in nearly every arena of modern life. In such a world, happiness was obviously a powerful commodity and one that would command our full attention.

Already by the middle of the twentieth century, people had largely given up on utopias. In their place came anti-utopias, such as George Orwell's *Nineteen Eighty-Four* and Aldous Huxley's *Brave New World*, that addressed the totalitarian control underlying the modern 'air-conditioned nightmare'. Gradually we were getting the message that the happy masses had been sold a shoddy bill of emotional goods. More recently, films like *The Matrix* and *The Truman Show* offer images of a completely false world that includes manufactured emotion to keep people 'happy' and usefully connected to the system. Art in general had turned itself away from utopia and happiness as we entered the second half of the twentieth century. This symbolised the state of happiness that existed at this time.

Happiness Key

Art teaches nothing except the significance of life.

– HENRY MILLER

Art is one of the last things that comes to mind today in discussions of what makes people happy. But from the dawn of our history, it has been a powerful, shared emotional language that could resurrect the spirit and activate the imagination as it spoke to us about the significance of life, as well as its beauties and dramas. Art was often a way of life for most people within a community. For instance, all Navajos were singers, and the majority of them composed songs. Very few Navajo men and women failed to develop artistic skills in areas such as sandpainting, silverwork, pottery, basketmaking, or the poetic use of language. They would not have known what to make of today's artists. Their hearts would have gone out to our small pool of dejected fringe-dwelling artists whose main hope for being recognised by the disinterested and artistically illiterate public is death. Until recently, art was inseparable from quality and skill. Even ordinary people could exercise their natural artistic leanings by way of the traditional crafts that were of practical as well as aesthetic importance. One can still see examples of this, such as the quality quiltwork and embroidery of Mennonite women who pass down this art form, which is usually done in groups, from one generation to the next. For them and other cultures over the ages, art and beauty were closely coupled. So too were art and happiness.

But by the 1930s, art had set itself on a course of expressing the narcissism and alienation that was in the ascendancy in modern consumer culture. It would lose much of its ability to speak to the emotions, and to our aesthetic instincts, which is clearly the case with all forms of contemporary art. Today, the main criterion for worthwhile art is that it is different or new. We have come to accept as art such monstrosities as a dead shark in a tank of formaldehyde, shirts in a can, and a straight line in a sealed tube. Urinals, street signs, garbage bins, or nail clippings will do as well. As a language, art has become so garbled that it is no longer easy to think of it as a contributor to human happiness.

Yet this is exactly the point according to some defenders of contemporary art. They argue that the apparent lack of quality and craftsmanship is actually designed to demolish happiness in its present form, and to muster a challenge to a culture of illusion and unfounded positivity. In a sense, ugly art is seen as a necessary but foul-tasting medicine for an ugly form of happiness. This is a somewhat different interpretation from that in which unartistic art is seen simply as a direct mirror of the ugliness and meaninglessness that has engulfed contemporary society.

In his *Time* magazine article 'The Art of Unhappiness', James Poniewozik writes that the rise of 'anti-happy art' has more to do with the horribly large quantity of happiness: 'The reason may be that there is too much damn happiness in the world today.' However, he adds that this happiness into which we have been goaded by the mass media is a bogus variety that lacks much potential for real happiness. In part, the war that he sees between modern art and happiness may have the eventual effect of directing our attention away from 'easy happiness', as he calls it, and toward the sobering truth that loss, pain, sacrifice, and disappointment are the grounds from which happiness grows. Poniewozik concludes in saying 'We need art to tell us, as religion once did, *Memento mori*: remember that you will die, that everything ends, and that happiness comes not in denying this but in living it.'

Whether or not modern art actually began trying to combat 'the tyranny of the positive attitude', as philosopher William James called it, one thing was certain. Like everything else, happiness was becoming increasingly commercialised. Consciousness itself was coming under the increasing control of economic forces, with sociologists speaking of the new 'economic being' and some renaming our species *homo economicus*. By the late 1980s we had become emotionally dilapidated marketing characters. But happiness had become an indispensable fashion accessory. It was essential to wear the look of a happy person. The 'say cheese' phenomenon would help to gloss over the deteriorating inner worlds of *homo economicus*.

The history of photography, which begins with the first photographic image in 1826, parallels to some extent the modern history of happiness. If you browse through photographs from the nineteenth century, you will not see any 'say cheese' smiles or happy faces. The same is true with our ancestors in the early twentieth century, where there are still no happy faces. It was alright to look sombre, melancholic, or pensive. Even today in most non-Western societies people feel no need to give a false picture of their emotional state when a camera is pointed their way. The concept of life as a series of contrived 'Kodak moments' has not yet sunk in there.

Some photographic historians explain this simply in terms of the slow shutter speed of early cameras, saying it was probably harder to hold a smile than a flat expression. This could account for part of the phenomenon. But there is also a strong sociological factor as well. Most people can in fact hold a smile steady enough for a prolonged exposure. The great nineteenth-century photographer Félix Tournachon Nadar used to say that he sought to capture the 'moral intelligence' of his subjects. This was possible in a social climate that had not yet imposed a taboo on non-happiness. It was still acceptable to view life through a lens of reality in which suffering, death, and loss was an inevitable part of the human story. A solemn and weighty 'Elizabethan' demeanour was not considered the sign of a failed life.

Before happiness became obligatory as a fashion statement, one could even stand tall with a look of cynicism, doubt, and resignation. None of this meant that something was wrong, or in need of repair. That was life. There was nothing shameful about portraying oneself in a manner suggesting that one was not having fun. Presenting oneself with dignity was a much stronger drive in the early days of photography. Today the happy face is social mascara that covers up new types of pain.

In the course of cultivating positivity, people found themselves engaged in a peculiar sort of interior decoration in which they painted over any emotions that could smudge the appearance of happiness. Just as it had been possible to hide emotionally from the reality of death, the emerging social structure was making it easier to hide from the experience of a wide range of emotions. This included ones that were fused with life itself, such as sadness and sorrow. Swiss psychologist Carl Jung voiced very well the need to keep oneself open to all emotions – even the dark ones – in order to preserve our ability to feel happiness: 'There are as many nights as days, and the one is just as long as the other in the year's course. Even a happy life cannot be without a measure of darkness, and the word "happy" would lose its meaning if it were not balanced by sadness.'

Happiness Key

The deeper that sorrow carves into your being, the more joy you can contain.

– KAHLIL GIBRAN

In constantly trying to cheer up ourselves and put on a happy face, we fail to create the spaces for happiness about which Lebanese poet Kahlil Gibran writes in *The Prophet*. No one is less capable of sustaining happiness than someone who is singularly set on feeling only happiness. It explains why 'savages' were happier than those who discovered them, and why happiness is in so much more abundance in societies where forces are in place that compete with happiness. The capacity to be happy depends on our ability to feel things other than happiness.

Going into the twenty-first century, people would have to find happiness among a cultural ruins in which all the major human needs had been frustrated, with the exception of material ones that were being saturated. Society was becoming colder. The world was filling with noise, congestion, and unprecedented levels of distrust. The heart, mind, body, and soul were all under siege. Happiness had become a matter of 'each man for himself'. The story of happiness, as well as modern life generally, had become one reflected perfectly in the title of Bryce Courtenay's book *The Power of One*. There is no better epitaph for social happiness, and no better motto for the challenge facing modern people.

Solitary heroics were the bugle call for millions of one-person armies that were mustering on their own borders, ready to conquer an angry world that was increasingly at odds with happiness. As cogs in an economic machine, people found themselves whipped by new and more radical forms of competition that kept pointing them toward busyness. There came a point when they were too busy to conceive of happiness as something that required them to work on themselves, or to improve the messy world in any way. This opened up the gate for an instant happiness that came merely by wishing for it.

The new wand that could be waved was 'choice'. This was a type of mental magic that could override past learning, social issues, cultural indoctrination, biology, temperament, unconscious conflicts, prevailing circumstances, and life's realities. Choice was the quick emotional face-lift that was sought by the stressed and depressed masses that had nothing of themselves to invest in happiness. It became the supreme trump card. To this day, choice is power. All one has to do is to choose, or 'decide', that one wants to be happy. The choice revolution has even infiltrated the offices of counsellors and psychotherapists where one finds the words 'choice' and 'choose' at the top of the latest list of jargon.

Just as people are instructed that they can choose not to be depressed, they are told that they can choose to be happy. The logic behind it is simple, even infantile. As in a child's fairy tale, one merely wishes for it to come true. With the evolution of happiness-by-choice, all former labour-intensive approaches to happiness seemed a nonsensical waste of time. One now wonders how people in the past could have been so blind to the happiness express lane.

Choosing happiness became no more difficult than making a decision about white versus wholewheat bread. Wholewheat is healthier than white, so I choose wholewheat. Happy is better than unhappy, so I choose happy. Today this happiness-for-dummies trend is reflected in the piles of new books that have hit the bookshelves. People cannot seem to get filled up on the scintillating promise of effortless choice, even if it only delivers a thin veneer of happiness.

Several books have come out in the past few years with the title *Choose to Be Happy*. The same is true with the title *Happiness Is a Choice*. Every other combination of 'happy' and 'choice' has been used in still other books about the miraculous powers of choice; for example, *How We Choose to Be Happy*, *Happiness through Choice*, *How to Choose Your Happy Ending*, and *Joy Choice: Happiness Is an Inside Job*. Many other books instruct the reader how to use choice for more than just happiness. For instance, *Choose to Be Fit, Healthy, and Happy*. If you are still depressed after this, there are also books such as Arline Curtis's *Depression Is a Choice*. If you are not sure how to actually start choosing, some of these books will tell you that, like everything else, you choose to choose.

We now find ourselves as far away as possible from the classical vision of happiness as the pinnacle of an arduous climb. The tables have been turned completely. Happiness is now the starting point. A few simple techniques will get you there. This complete reversal can be seen in the ways that many happiness coaches pitch their wares.

For instance, one British happiness coach advertises his service by pointing out that 'throughout the world millions of people suffer from loneliness, self-doubt, failure, anger, frustration and misery'. He then says that the reason for this is because they lack the understanding that 'you cannot build a happy life without happiness'. The only thing that can bring happiness, he adds, is to first make yourself happy. In other words, unhappiness is caused by a lack of happiness.

Happiness has lost all its prerequisites. There is no longer a honeymoon period. In a similar way to which we now view fame and wealth, we can now start very close to the finish line. The reasoning is warped, but this drive-through mode of happiness accommodates itself nicely with the economic gods that rule the modern world.

CHAPTER NINE

The Happiness Conspiracy

JOHN Updike's famous quote 'America is a vast conspiracy to make you happy' comes from his short story 'How to Love America and Leave It at the Same Time'. It is about a traveller who put up for the night in a small, lifeless American town. In the midst of his boredom, he began reflecting on the commercial wasteland that surrounded him on all sides. It struck him that all former roads had been redirected toward marketed banalities: 'To acquire substance, enter a store and buy something.'

Updike – who elsewhere writes 'Happiness is not the ally but the enemy of the truth' – describes the people of this town as ones who had sold out their souls and their happiness to trinkets and death. Armies of salespeople kept close guard so no one went unquenched for even a moment, lest he or she might be tempted to feel something other than satisfaction. After all, he realised, 'This is America, where we take everything in.' To find happiness, gulp something. Happiness, and America itself, seemed to be modelling itself on the fast-food industry: 'America, a hamburger kingdom, one cuisine, under God, indivisible, with pickles and potato chips for all.' You might love it, but you have to leave.

Writer J. D. Salinger also smelled a cultural rat that led him to say 'I am a kind of paranoiac in reverse. I suspect people are plotting to make one happy.' At heart, every culture is a conspiracy to keep its members 'happy' in the sense that they willingly and unquestioningly obey its norms. Cultures are living organisms that fight to stay alive, just like any other form of life. Norms are the building blocks of culture. For a culture to survive, these norms must be followed. In *Mr Sammler's Planet*, Saul Bellow warns about the dangers of seeking happiness against the norms of society: 'Happiness is to do what most people do. Just don't contradict your time. Just don't contradict it, that's all.'

All cultures evolve emotional systems to reward people for their conformity. They make sure that adherence to norms carries enough positive emotional payoff to outweigh any negatives that stem from obedience. Every society has its seers and critics who, like John Updike's character, catch on to the conspiracy and stage a minor rebellion against their own 'happiness'. But even a hamburger kingdom offers enough tasty pickles and potato chips to make the whole enterprise palatable to most.

We like to think that we are lords of our own fate and governors of our own happiness. But almost everybody is spurred along primarily by the urge to be normal. No one described the sweet tragedy of normality better than Peter Schaffer who writes in *Equus* 'Normal is the good smile in a child's eye, and also the dead stare in a million adults. It both sustains and kills like a god. Normal is the indispensable murderous god of health.' The god that we call culture determines the general direction of happiness and sets up road signs of all sorts to keep us on track. In this regard, happiness is largely defined by cultural norm-ality. But when the god becomes crazy, and begins to point us in the wrong directions for authentic happiness, there may be no option but to distance ourselves from its norms and values, however difficult that might be.

All indications suggest that modern consumer culture has become insane due to the fact that its patterns of indoctrination are causing the majority of people to become so removed from their core human needs that serious problems are being caused in terms of mental health, social well-being, physical fitness, and planetary survival. But despite this, it still manages to convince most people that they are happy. If this can be called a conspiracy, it is an effective one that disguises the emotional deadness that is the signature of modern life.

The psychic deadness that was generated by the society in Huxley's *Brave New World* was kept safely from people's awareness by a happiness drug known as 'soma'. It produced a superficial mass happiness that revolved around sensory self-indulgence. Completely manufactured, it managed to prevent people from becoming concerned or informed about the nature of the deprivations that they needed to bear in order to be normal in that inhuman environment. The comparisons today are more than obvious.

The barrage of images that shape our consciousness can have a powerful cumulative effect on even the most intelligent people. They can be very effective at attaching the notion of happiness to products and services that have nothing whatsoever to do with being happy. This process is referred to in the advertising industry as 'emotional branding'. I recently saw an advertisement headline that read 'I can make you feel good' and underneath that were the words 'Red Meat'. The images in which we are awash can also implant the false perception that there is a gold mine of happiness that has been discovered by other people, but not ourselves. Usually we would have the reality checks to dismiss all these images as nonsense. But as we have become increasingly deprived of honest communication with other people, we find ourselves with fewer and fewer ways to dispel these images, as well as the overall myth of a happy world.

So what is the problem? One could argue that a television commercial showing a blissfully happy family – even if it was a new polluting and wasteful sport utility vehicle that made them so happy – would serve to lift people's spirits, and even make them a tinge happier. Should not the same thing occur when looking at a radiantly happy face in a magazine or newspaper, even if it was a new bikini brief or deodorant that brought the results? After all, the theory behind the original happy face back in 1963 was that people, especially miserable ones, would be cheered up by happy images. Unfortunately, the opposite is the case.

Modern times have witnessed a titanic collision of happy images and depression. Research has found that simple happy images, such as the happy face, trigger a chain of brain reactions that amplify depression in depressed people, as well as depression-prone ones. I recall a depressed psychotherapy patient of mine who told me during one session that even a brief glimpse of the Wiggles – a music group for children that takes the happy look to where no one has gone before – triggered in him a surge of anger followed by worsened depression. Reactions like this are not totally unexpected in light of the fact that misery loves company. But it is not only the many millions of depressed people who are being persecuted by happy images. Studies have found that non-depressed people also suffer negative emotional consequences by repeated exposures to images of others who ooze with happiness. Most theories trying to explain this say that successive images of extravagant happiness erode one's self-concept by way of comparison. Not only do we perceive ourselves to be inferior in the happiness stakes, but we realise that we could never reach the emotional heights of those being idealised in the images. The resulting deflation is bred by an accumulation of self-perceived failures.

Another explanation revolves around a stirring-up of envy, which has also been shown to be associated with depression and feelings of worthlessness. In either case, it seems only natural that incessant exposure to happy images has prompted many people to wear a sunny disposition, even if it is a mask. This too has created potentially depressing conditions for people who simply do not have sunny dispositions, or those whose integrity is offended by pretence.

The swamp of images depicting people whose radiant happiness is the result of a purchase helps serve as a type of propaganda about the wonders of consumer capitalism. In her book *Selling Happiness*, Ellen Johnston Laing describes how poster art in communist China, which showed rapturously happy comrades serving the state, functioned to indoctrinate people into believing that they were happy with communism. The endless counterparts of these posters in contemporary society have a similar propaganda effect. But in addition to equating acts of consumption with happiness, they carry the underlying message that we are not yet happy since we do not have what is being held out to us.

Rather than a simple conspiracy to make people happy, consumer culture is primarily interested in generating discontent, which is the basic operating principle of consumer capitalism. Discontent is the state of mind that current indoctrinations are designed to achieve. In this respect, today's people find themselves in a unique situation. On the one hand, happiness has become the Holy Grail that has seized everyone's attention. It is everywhere, but nowhere. On the other hand, they are being exposed to relentless programming that strives to unsettle people and keep them sufficiently discontented in order to remain robust consumers.

The commercialisation of our mental space may appear harmless. On the surface, it seems designed merely to pique our interest in one or more of the infinity of products, gadgets, and gizmos that compete so aggressively for our cash. But as Anna White of the Center for a New American Dream points out in her essay 'Selling Discontent', unhappiness in the form of discontent is the engine driving consumer culture and its people. She cites a former advertising executive who described the god-like power of advertising to eat a black hole of discontent into its targets: 'Next to Christianity, advertising is the greatest force in the world. And I say that without sacrilege or disrespect. Advertising makes people discontented. It makes them want things they don't have. Without discontent, there is no progress, no achievement.' Media advertising operates as a subtle form of emotional terrorism that instils doubts, fears, and inadequacy. It creates an intense yearning for solutions to the unrest that it creates.

Discontent has become so tightly woven into the fabric of our personalities that many people have lost virtually all capacity for sustained peace of mind. But the all-pervasive discontent industry provides both the problem and the solution. It trains us to be dissatisfied with ourselves and what we have by way of telling us what we lack. At the same time, it shows us how to remedy our deficiencies by way of the right commercial choices. However, no person has the financial means or time to plug up the endless holes in our lives that are pointed out to us. We can shrug off most of these false alarms if we think about them consciously. But there are simply too many of them for us to avoid a residual feeling of failure.

Happiness Key

Contentment is a pearl of great price, and whoever procures it at the expense of ten thousand desires makes a wise and a happy purchase.

– John Balguy

Contentment is a true form of luxury. But it is no longer well understood. Contentment has been cursed many times, especially in recent decades when it has become a threat to consumer economics. Often it is attacked as a stagnant state of complacency. But quite the reverse, it is an active system that allows a person to extract meaning, purpose, and direction from a realistically sized slice of life. Contentment is a form of strength. But discontent is never far from fear. It is founded on ignorance and illusion. People who succumb to discontent are condemned to the experience of futility. They never arrive at a place that feels like home. They are the real homeless people of the world. But the discontented make fabulous consumers.

Happiness Key

Be happy with what you have and are, be generous with both, and you won't have to hunt for happiness.

– William E. Gladstone

William Gladstone, the nineteenth-century British Prime Minister, realised that contentment could defuse the fruitless quest for happiness. Interestingly, it does not matter how much one has, or how fortunate one is. People adapt very quickly to what they have. They then begin to compare themselves to other people, or media images of people, who have more. Therefore, being 'fortunate' is completely relative. Even a billionaire surrounded by luxuries of every sort can feel deprived. People who are joining the many 'luxury clubs' that are springing up around the world seem to be missing the point. Material possessions, no matter how luxurious, offer no psychological end point at which they can step off. People come to take what they have for granted, while continually increasing the baseline for what they feel will finally make them happy. The initial thrill of a new Toyota soon fades into a vague sense that a BMW or Mercedes would better satisfy their car needs. But it is a road that never leads away from discontent.

As Socrates walked through a bazaar one day, he was struck by how little he needed materially in order to be happy. 'What a lot of things I do not need,' he proclaimed. He saw the wisdom of being able to eliminate false needs from one's life, since this avoids wasting one's energy on goals that offer nothing positive emotionally. In *Be Merry, Friends*, sixteenth-century British dramatist John Heywood smears wealth as a magnet for false needs, while advising pauperism as a better source of happiness.

> The loss of wealth is loss of dirt,
> As sages in all times assert;
> The happy man's without a shirt.

Heywood did not mean 'without a shirt' in any literal sense of the word. Abject poverty in which survival needs go unmet is a ticket to misery. But there is a higher meaning of the word 'poor' that has a long Christian tradition. The Beatitude 'Blessed are the poor in spirit, for theirs is the kingdom of heaven' is the source of considerable confusion, especially for modern people who have nothing but negative associations with the concept of poorness. The biblical meaning of the word 'blessed' was 'happy' or 'to be envied'. To be 'poor' in the original Christian way is to transcend material acquisitiveness. Conversely, greed is seen as the sin that clouds the path to spiritual enlightenment and a state of grace. The 'blissfulness of the poor' of which some religious scholars speak comes from the profound understanding that one is nothing in the greater scheme of things.

Being 'poor' in this higher sense bestows humility and counteracts tendencies toward selfishness. It can be a positive type of 'destitution' that frees us to turn our gaze to loftier matters. In this poverty, which can be self-imposed, we help guard ourselves from external elements that weigh people down to a frivolous existence. It constrains self-glorification and makes easier such self-transcending emotions as love, compassion, and trust. Our wealth has grown considerably in recent decades. But it has become dirt for so many people who are using it in a way that blinds them to the poorness and simplicity in which a nourishing happiness lies.

The 'before' and 'after' images that feature in many ads are designed specifically to illustrate a product's ability to transform unhappiness into happiness. The 'before' person is invariably slump-shouldered and frowning. The 'after' person is rejuvenated and glowing. The tone of commercial indoctrinations creates fears that one is the dreaded 'before' person. Simultaneously, it sparks desire to achieve the 'after' state.

Desire is a big part of the equation for holding people hostage to a customer approach to happiness. Aside from stirring up fears that translate into discontent, consumer culture has become a finely tuned instrument that can create new desires, and amplify existing ones. As soon as one desire is satisfied, another takes its place and demands recognition. Dream merchants who are benefiting from the happiness boom have created sophisticated marketing technologies that can root out and inflate every potential desire.

The well-known lyrics 'I can't get no satisfaction' by the Rolling Stones easily qualifies as the official anthem of consumer culture. Yet in the midst of the impossibility of being satisfied, there is a lot of satisfying going on. In an odd sort of way, modern people are always in the process of being satisfied. However, they are also never satisfied because each satisfied desire is quickly replaced by a new one that seizes their attention. They extinguish one emotional bush fire, and feel good about that momentarily, but then notice that there are others burning to which they must run. If you step into their inferno and ask if they are 'satisfied', they are likely to say 'yes' due to a lifestyle that revolves around satisfaction. But in reality the person is ping-ponging back and forth between satisfaction and the new itches that are arriving at all times.

To say that the average person in consumer culture is 'satisfied' is a virtual absurdity. Discontent is too large a part of our experience. It is what keeps alive the American Dream, and the pursuit of consumer happiness. The interplay of desire and discontent is a perfect format for a cultural system that has assigned its fate to overconsumption. If the masses were happy in the sense of being truly contented, the wheels would fall off the runaway locomotive of consumer capitalism.

Desire is as old as civilisation itself, and so are its potential pitfalls. It takes self-discipline to keep control over desire. Yet many thinkers, especially ones from Eastern schools of thought, have seen this as the first step toward genuine happiness. This is especially important in an age when desire threatens to rupture the essence of our beings. Master Hsing Yun summarises the Buddhist view on healthy versus unhealthy desire.

> Realise that excessive desire causes suffering. Healthy desires include reasonable hunger, a balanced pursuit of shelter and clothing, reasonable social activity, temperate sexuality, and a balanced pursuit of hobbies or other amusements. Excessive desire means going beyond these parameters. When we exceed them, we cause suffering. Reasonable desires do not preoccupy us, and they are not distracting or extreme. If we do not fulfil them, we do not feel that they cannot wait a little longer. Excessive desires strain our health, impair our concentration, and often cause us to become angry or envious.

As this suggests, Buddhism does not see the happy person as one who has extinguished all desire. Instead, happiness is thought to reside in 'The Middle Way', which is the term used by Buddha to describe the healthy halfway point between denial and overindulgence. No desire should become so strong that it becomes the centrepoint of a person's life and dilutes their ability to concentrate on the goals of wisdom, kindness, and enlightenment. The three states that come closest to sin in Buddhist philosophy – greed, ignorance, and anger – are all thought to be encouraged by immoderate levels of desire. Hindu philosophy teaches that excessive desire interferes with deeper forms of awareness that are essential to achieve knowledge of the Supreme Soul, which is the source of eternal bliss.

Happiness Key

'Well,' said Pooh, 'what I like best—' and then
he had to stop and think. Because although
Eating Honey was a very good thing to do,
there was a moment just before you began to
eat it which was better than when you were,
but he didn't know what it was called.

— A. A. MILNE

In this delightful passage from *Winnie the Pooh*, Pooh makes one of his greatest accidental discoveries when he realises that the moment before eating honey tastes better than the honey itself. He does not know a word for it, but we could easily call it happiness. Milne had a fine eye for the subtle textures of human happiness. Some of these he saw as residing in our ability to befriend nature, the deepest well of happiness. For example, he has Eeyore the donkey, one of Pooh's chums, express this by way of a defence of the humble weed: 'Weeds are flowers too, once you get to know them.'

Keeping some desire alive may offer more prospects for happiness than the constant consummation of desire, and this is probably the case. Cicero saw the wisdom of holding back from swallowing when he said 'Happiness exists in desire rather than fulfilment.'

The sexuality-based Hindu philosophy of Tantra, sometimes called the 'Science of Ecstasy', teaches that the greatest bliss lies in a sacred awareness of desire itself. Dating to the fourth century, it illuminates the emotional and spiritual beauty of resisting the urge to consummate sexual urges, which is why they emphasise 'dry orgasms' and other methods of preventing final climax.

As with happiness, desire is being understood as a state that one consumes. It would spell economic disaster in a consumer society if people began to relish the tantalising state of suspension that precedes the destruction of the desire. The preferred type of consumer is one who has been honed to hop, skip, and jump as quickly as possible from one consuming desire to the next, without pausing to savour along the way.

Happiness Key

To be without some of the things you want is an indispensable part of happiness.

— BERTRAND RUSSELL

These words were spoken by Bertrand Russell as he was telling about people who can be unhappy despite having everything. A certain degree of deprivation keeps alive one's prospects for happiness and optimism. Consider the unfortunate people whose houses have magnificent views. Almost inevitably, they habituate to it within a matter of weeks or months, and then fail to be moved by it any longer. The same is true with swimming pools. If you want to find people who are incapable of screaming for joy as they take the plunge, just look for ones who have a big fancy pool in their backyards. You are unlikely to even see them in the pool, much less find it a potent source of enjoyment.

It is always unwise to try to wrap heaven around oneself. Happiness is a brush of white against a black canvas, a moment of sunshine on a cloudy day, a flower in the desert, all of which must threaten to vanish. Humanistic psychologist Rollo May once said 'One cannot love without death.' Maybe a similar thing is true of happiness. Its life is dependent upon its potential mortality. Keeping paradise at a distance, yet within reach, is usually a much better way of staying alive. People who have it all must make a special effort to learn the art of flirting with deprivation.

Faulty 'emotional forecasting' is one factor that incites people to pounce, boots and all, on every desire. It is a common shortcoming. A number of researchers have discovered that most of us are dismal failures when it comes to predicting how happy we will be, or how long we will be made happy, by the things that we choose to consume. We expect far more happiness from leather car seats, designer bathrooms, and extra-wide surround-sound plasma televisions than they are able to fulfil.

Contributing to our flawed ability to forecast the happiness impact of material products is the marketing industry's ability to pump us full of hope regarding various products. In this regard, the background of repeated disappointments that accompanies the pursuit of material happiness often stems from people having too much hope. We usually think of hope as something that is always healthy. But hope that is doomed to be dashed never added anything to happiness. Novelist Henry Miller touches on this in *Tropic of Cancer* where he writes 'I have no money, no resources, no hopes. I am the happiest man alive.'

CHAPTER TEN

In Greed We Trust

ONE of the most famous concepts in the history of psychology is Abraham Maslow's 'hierarchy of needs'. His basic theory was that human beings are naturally inclined to shift attention to higher-level needs (i.e. social, intellectual, and spiritual ones) once we have satisfied our lower-level needs for food, shelter, and the material things required for survival. By moving on from fulfilled lower needs, he said, we can channel our motivation toward beauty, truth, affection, belongingness, honour, respect, appreciation, and dignity, all traits that characterise the 'self-actualised' person.

Maslow might be correct in his basic assumption that human beings are upwardly driven and that we will not by nature persist in trying to satisfy low-level needs once they are satisfied. But consumer culture has become extremely good at persuading people to remain fixated upon their material needs, even though they have been satisfied many times over. The reason for this is simply that low-level needs offer much greater scope for consumption, which is why consumer culture resists this upward movement, and strives to keep people incomplete, undeveloped, and unhappy in terms of our full potential as human beings.

The gourmet water phenomenon highlights one way in which we can keep spinning our wheels with needs that are already satisfied. We need water. That would be one of the lowest-level needs at the bottom of Maslow's hierarchy of human needs. Many modern Western societies have safe drinking water. For those with water purity problems, there are relatively inexpensive sources of bottled water, or ways of filtering it at home. This makes it a perfect opportunity to forget about that need and to get a life, so to speak.

But a huge and growing economic gravity tries to keep us riveted to the issue of water. The multi-billion-dollar deluxe bottled water industry has transformed the need for water into a quest for luxury and status. The millions of people who have bought into the manufactured need for 'premium' water are discussing the pros and cons of virtuoso waters like Gerolsteiner, Badoit, Jagger's, or Evian. An entire vocabulary has evolved to capture the subtle differences in carbonation levels and mineral content.

Water bars are appearing, and water hot spots like the Ritz-Carlton in New York City even have a specially trained water sommelier to guide one's difficult choices from their vast premium water list. The very chic water bars even carry Kona Nigari sea water that sells for US$35 for two ounces. Exotic glass bottles of every colour and variety are prompting some people to become avid collectors, with highly sought-after ones fetching several hundred dollars. Books are on offer that catalogue and describe the top waters of the world. Courses on 'aqua tasting' are attracting large numbers of budding water connoisseurs.

The enjoyment once found in a simple cup of plain coffee

has now been commercialised away and thrust onto an escalator of ever more extravagant concoctions that require one to stay boned up on the coffee culture vocabulary. Instead of being allowed to move on from the marvellous double-edged razor, triple-edged razors were pushed at us, and now quadruple-edged ones are rushing in to ensure that we stay occupied with facial hair. The conspirators are unrelenting.

The toothbrush, once a humble and inexpensive tool for cleaning teeth, has entered the realm of science fiction. We must now choose from dozens of bizarre-looking devices, some purple and translucent with swirly rippled interfaces between ergonomically-designed handles and micro-heads, and others with sharp bends, transparent handles with a kaleidoscope of glitter, rubber prongs, and clumsy, multi-directional brush heads. Toothbrushes are also attracting strong interest from collectors, especially designer ones like the African Safari toothbrush, or celebrity ones such as the Barbie, Hulk, and Spiderman brushes. Like water, there is plenty of scope to stay happy at the level of the toothbrush. The same is true of thousands of objects related to low-level needs that have been jazzed up in order to keep our heads in the consumer gutter.

In many ways, the same thing has happened to happiness as to toothbrushes, water, running shoes, and razors. It has become elaborated out of proportion, hyped up, promoted, and sold as a commodity. Ordinary offerings are being constantly refined and made more sophisticated so we do not need to turn our gaze upwards. The pursuit of happiness is becoming the pursuit of the trivial.

There is a trend among happiness coaches to pitch happiness as a form of 'mental wealth' that can be accumulated like money or material possessions. The similar concept of 'emotional abundance' has translated into books and workshops on the subject of becoming filthy rich with happiness. One such happiness workshop in the UK promotes itself on the grounds that 'emotional abundance teaches you how to experience more of what you really want', as if people do not want enough already. Even if people have an unconscious yearning to address their higher needs, consumer culture is designed to fence people in to a materially defined happiness that is beneath them. Its goal is to limit their aspirations for happiness to the realm of whatever can be consumed.

Materialism is defined as 'a cultural system in which material interests are not made subservient to other social goals and in which material self-interest is pre-eminent'. It is a value system that has been rising rapidly over the past several decades since it is so good at cranking out itchy consumers. As this unfolds, people have come to believe that objects will make them happy. Many people still say that children, spouses, friends, and a stroll on the beach are the main sources of happiness. But they are no longer living their lives as if this were the case.

Actions speak louder than words when trying to locate the modern sources of happiness. Researchers are learning that it is more accurate to pay attention to the positive or negative impact of specific events throughout the day. Doing this gives a much different picture of happiness than surveys that ask people to rely on long-term memory and to make broad statements about what makes them happy. For example, women invariably put 'my children' at or near the top when they are asked to rank what gives them the greatest happiness. However, when the quality of their emotions is measured on a moment-by-moment basis throughout the day, 'looking after my children' comes way down on the list, alongside housework and cooking. One such study of 900 Texas women by Princeton University researcher Daniel Kahneman found that watching television and eating even rated far above the children when it came to good feelings.

We no longer live in a cultural system that directs us to value, and thus define our happiness, by way of parenthood, meaningful relationships, or a beautiful mind. With materialism becoming so dominant, it is understandable that people increasingly try to become happy by living in accordance with such values. But there are some ugly flies in the ointment of material happiness. The most basic one is that it is very costly to the well-being of the planet. Several studies have confirmed that people with strongly fixed materialistic values have diminished regard for nature, the environment, and ecological issues. In the course of pursuing happiness by way of material conquests, they appear to lose the ability to appreciate earthly wonders or to experience feelings of unity with nature. Societies full of happy materialists spell ecological doom.

But materialism does not lend itself easily to happiness. One reason is that money and material goods create a very low ceiling on happiness. The amount of ongoing satisfaction that can be derived from an income of $20,000 is virtually the same as can be derived from an annual income of $2,000,000 dollars. No amount of luxuries or pampering makes much difference to our happiness. All monetary overkill does is to raise the price of happiness. Of this, Mignon McLaughlin wrote in *The Neurotic's Notebook* that 'Happiness is like the penny candy of our youth. We got a lot more for our money when we had no money.' This is no great secret. A vast literature exists on this subject. No one any longer even bothers to argue that superfluous quantities of money or things make one happier. This has been one of the biggest myths in the modern happiness manifesto.

If there is an exception to this rule about money, it has

to do with the perception that one is the victim of extreme financial inequality. Research shows that people are less happy when the amount of money they make is conspicuously below the average amount within the same society. For this reason, greater overall levels of happiness tend to be found in societies that are egalitarian in nature. Problems arise in a country like America that is founded on economic principles that continually widen the gulf between people at opposite ends of the financial continuum. Those on the lower rungs of the ladder might have enough money for all the basics that are necessary for happiness. But their happiness is always being compromised because they were indoctrinated with needs and desires that cannot be afforded. They suffer from a form of relative deprivation whereby they are being reminded daily of what they do not have, and of what they feel they must have in order to be happy. The result is frustration.

Rage usually goes hand in hand with this relative sort of capitalistic unhappiness. It usually does not take much to send such societies spiralling into anarchy and lawlessness. If having lots of money in an unequally divided country can make some positive difference to happiness, it is again by virtue of contrasts. In America, there is a steady procession of relative 'have-nots' against whom one can compare oneself, if that is in fact how one is making oneself happy. But it is doubtful that this form of happiness contributes much to the emotional well-being of individuals. It is counterbalanced by the knowledge that it hangs from a thin thread, and that it is the product of a system that breeds hatred as it conspires to equate money with happiness.

Happiness Key

I can't afford to waste my time making money.

— LOUIS AGASSIZ

The great nineteenth-century Swiss-born scientist Louis Agassiz spoke the above words while discussing the wretchedness of lecturing for fees. As one of the founding fathers of the modern scientific tradition, money struck him as an irritating distraction that took his mind off of the more important matter of knowledge. Today, however, money is the stuff of dreams. Yet some recent studies have found that high levels of wealth can in some cases lead to decreased happiness. This was especially apparent among high-income earners who lived in exclusive neighbourhoods. Such people often have exceptionally high financial aspirations, a drive that research shows to be destructive to happiness. Children from high-income families living in upper-class neighbourhoods were found to be less happy and confident than children from middle-class neighbourhoods and even inner-city ghettos.

These sorts of findings are understood in terms of the unrealistic expectations that are spawned in environments in which people make careers out of excess. Having greater amounts of money can actually set off dissatisfaction that in turn fuels more desires. This is part of the tendency for high levels of wealth to dull people to what they have and to focus their attention on what they lack. This means that many rich people end up feeling more deprived than their less wealthy counterparts. Philosopher Eric Hoffer was on the mark when he said 'You can never get enough of what you don't need to make you happy.' Making matters worse is that the world of upper-class people is so entrenched in hyper-competition that it drowns most prospects for satisfying, intimate relationships.

As a personality trait, materialism has been shown by numerous studies to create obstacles to happiness. Among other things, a strong materialistic orientation has been associated with envy, narcissism, relationship problems, and a diminished ability to feel empathy for others. Materialists often view the body itself as an object that they can manipulate, renovate, or invest in like any other object. It is used to mop up pleasure and sensation, and to digest the goods and services that try in vain to simmer down our boiling appetites.

The body has become a wasteland from the standpoint of happiness and vitality. Eighty per cent of Americans are now overweight, with 45 per cent classified as clinically obese. Mixed in with this is a fat phobia epidemic that sees people punishing their bodies with every conceivable type of diet, workout contraption, and gymnasium programme, all of which is part of the voracious industry that feeds off our body preoccupations. Beyond that, the body is under siege from a fast-growing 'makeover' industry that tries to equate happiness with youth. It promises to implant, suck out, cut away, burn off, or redesign whatever parts it takes to make the person happier by way of physical appearance. But it has now become clear from research that physical makeovers have no permanent benefits in making over the person emotionally.

The human brain has also come under heavy attack as happiness has steadily come to be seen as something that can be consumed. The billion-dollar drug industries, both legal and illegal, that involve the peddling of endless types of 'happy pills' are a direct reflection of the rise of consumer happiness. In his

1898 work *Candida*, Irish playwright George Bernard Shaw writes 'We have no more right to consume happiness without producing it than to consume wealth without producing it.' But the merits of that wisdom have been lost in an age wherein we feel entitled to happiness even if we had no input into it.

A drug industry currently worth over 20 billion dollars annually has grown up around the phenomenon of Western depression. In fairness, millions of victims of the Age of Depression have found no relief from non-chemical treatments, or ones that ask them simply to choose away or think away their depression. Psychotherapy can be partially effective for many, but it has done nothing to cut down the number of depressed people in the West, or to prevent the epidemic from worsening. Thus, it is hard to argue that the depressed masses are not entitled to their fair share of the anti-depressant medications that are being handed out like Halloween candy.

Most popular are the Prozac-style SSRI drugs that have become for millions of mood-challenged individuals their first port of therapeutic call. Tens of millions of SSRI prescriptions are being given annually to people of the current chemical generation. Children are making up an increasingly large part of the depression industry. In 2003, around 15 million SSRI prescriptions were given to children and teenagers. But it does not appear to be stopping the descent of young people into depression, despair, and suicide.

Some critics have argued that this drugging trend is part of the reason for the rising numbers of youth suicides. They cite the many studies that have shown increased suicide potential to be a side-effect of SSRI use in children. But there are wider arguments against the trend toward viewing mood-altering drugs as part of the shopping spree mentality that has emerged in relation to the emotions. One of these is that the scurry to treat ourselves chemically is blocking the path to a natural happiness that flows on from a balanced and healthy life.

Depression should be telling us that something is out of kilter in our lives, which for a great many people is the case. Of this, health scientist James Prescott of the US National Institute of Health writes in *America's Lost Dream* that 'clearly something is wrong in our culture when our children and teens are driven to suicide, despair and [legal] drug addiction'. By whitewashing the real causes of modern misery with medication, we deprive ourselves of the chance to approach depression for what it really is, namely a social disease. In its place, we often end up with 'fake happiness', as it is sometimes called, which is actually one of the many side-effects that have been listed with the use of SSRI medication.

Profit-driven drug companies have done a masterful job of marketing not only their new drugs, but the diseases themselves. Never before have we had so many diseases with which to evaluate our well-being. It is hard to keep them all straight. There are now so many that normal states of mind are being confused with diseases. Non-happiness is one of these. Increasing numbers of people are showing up for medical visits, psychiatric consultations, and psychic readings with what can best be described as happiness anxiety. They are often not depressed, or even especially unhappy. But they are anxious that they are not as happy as they could be. Just under the surface is a fear that they are emotional losers.

Unhappiness has been repackaged as a disease. Normal levels of positive mood are being perceived increasingly as sub-normal. It is a peculiar variation of hypochondriasis that, for lack of a better term, could be called happichondriasis. In hypochondriasis, it is often some of the healthiest people who are preoccupied that something is wrong physically. Similarly, with the happichondriac, the happiness anxiety is often completely irrational given their circumstances and their actual level of experienced happiness. Yet they are convinced that something is deficient on the happiness front, or at least that it could be better if the right prescription was given.

While anti-depressant medication is inappropriate for people who judge themselves to be happiness deficient, many persist until they get a chemical fixer. This is part of the trend toward the use of 'lifestyle drugs' that spawns from the collective belief that people have a right to feel good at all times. Pharmaceutical companies are investing heavily in this rapidly growing market and are happy to do whatever it takes to sell people on the idea that, with their help, life can be a luxury emotional cruise without any foul winds. The question remains whether this and other doctored emotions can be called happiness.

The term 'negative happiness' is used sometimes to describe the type of happiness that does not allow the person to rise above an infantile material happiness that flows on from the satisfaction of fatuous wants and desires. In *Happiness and the Limits of Satisfaction*, Deal Hudson uses the term 'self-deceiving happiness' to describe the present-day commercialised type of happiness that increasingly is being used 'for the justification of self-centred and self-absorbed lives'. While this may fulfil the needs of a society that measures itself by gross domestic product, it leaves individuals feeling hollow, even if they are 'happy'.

Greed is now the strongest motive operating in modern culture. We have placed our collective trust in it, even though greed keeps happiness out of our reach by way of its unending requirement for more. The final frontier for greed is the emotions. People are being enticed to stuff their jowls with as much cheap candy-coated feelings as possible, even if it results in a sort of emotional obesity that numbs one to the subtle delicacies of life.

Chinese philosopher Lao Tzu wrote 2500 years ago that 'there is no calamity greater than lavish desires, no greater guilt than discontentment, and no greater disaster than greed'. But while greed may be a disaster from various standpoints including happiness, it is the fire in the belly of consumer economics, and thus the main goal of its indoctrinations. Many economists agree that greed is by far the best psychological launch pad for consumer activity, with some pointing out that greed is gradually being redefined as a virtue. There does in fact seem to be a good argument that greed is ideally suited for our current socio-economic structures.

We often think that human beings are greedy by nature. But as Judith Ann Johnson showed in her ground-breaking doctoral dissertation, greed is primarily determined by culture, despite whatever innate tendencies toward greediness we might have. She found that maximal greed was produced by a combination of capitalism, materialism, hyper-competition, and discrimination. The presence of all these today has made greed the master plan of economic growth and what she calls the 'map of Western consciousness'. Another part of her study found that greed receives additional fuel in societies that do not offer easy access to wisdom, inner awareness, and global understanding. The 'dumbing down' that we hear about so often with regard to consumer culture is actually a valuable strategy that sparks greed economics.

Greed makes for a happy economy in several specific ways. It suppresses the savings rate by way of ceaseless yearnings for all things consumable, which translates into ill-considered spending and a voracious appetite for credit. There is a famous economic formula that states 'for every 1 per cent rise in savings, corporate profits fall by 11 per cent'. If greed-inspired overspending in the United States would ease to the point that savings rose to a modest 5 per cent from their current sub-zero mark, corporate profits would fall by a blistering 50 per cent or more.

Greed supports the 'philosophy of more' that in turn keeps alive the 'big is beautiful' mentality. This spurs the market for profitable big-ticket items such as mini-mansions, four-wheel drive SUVs, and luxury playthings. Greed is the boiler room for the investment-driven booms in property, equity markets, and collectables. It generates enormous economic activity by way of speculation on everything from art to pork bellies. The gluttonous aspect of greed-mindedness also holds short-term advantages by way of increased tendencies toward waste, overconsumption, premature disposal and replacement, needless upgrading, and a general disregard for conservation.

The most dedicated greed enthusiasts even argue that greed's many economic payoffs outweigh the pitfalls pointed out by critics. These include the commercialisation of children, unhealthy levels of materialism, avarice, self-preoccupation, and irresponsible marketing that has led to health problems such as childhood obesity, diabetes, caffeine addiction among young people, and so forth. They ignore claims that unrestrained greed destroys equality, erodes freedom, and becomes an undemocratic force that leads to an apartheid economy. The one area where greed enthusiasts fall silent is the devastating effects that greed is having on the environment.

Happiness Key

The more he cast away the more he had.

– JOHN BUNYAN

These words are part of a short riddle from John Bunyan's famous seventeenth-century work *Pilgrim's Progress*. Several people are sitting around in someone's house cracking nuts when an old gentleman challenges the others to figure out the riddle 'a man there was, tho' some did count him mad, the more he cast away the more he had'. The discussion that followed was about the backwards nature of greed and how it has the unwanted final result of robbing the person of true wealth, whereas the real pot of gold lies within giving away: 'There is that maketh himself Rich, yet hath nothing, there is that maketh himself Poor, yet hath great Riches.' Samuel, one of the people solving the riddle that day, was so illuminated that he decided to stay in the house until his greedy brother beside him was 'married to Mercy'.

Philosopher Friedrich Nietzsche once commented on greed by saying 'he who cannot give anything away cannot feel anything either'. His words have proven to be true as greed has risen to glory. We are no longer feeling many of the emotions that we once felt. Mercy, compassion, conscience, love, reason, and community commitment are some of the things that are disappearing rapidly in our culture of greed. The rise of anti-intellectualism and the swallowing of higher education by the business community is also a consequence of greed culture.

Greed, it seems, is not nearly as good for human happiness as it is for the economy. Psychologists have begun using the label 'pleonexia' to diagnose pathological greed that contributes to a host of ills, including stress, burnout, addictions, 'affluenza', compulsive shopping/spending, 'possession obsession', and loss of moral grounding. The culture of greed also takes a serious toll on marriages, families, and the emotion of love generally.

The challenge facing the person trying so hard to be happy in today's world is that their happiness must somehow coexist with the toxic consequences of materialism, greed, and discontent. Narcissism is another millstone that consumer culture has strapped to the backs of people running the race to be happy.

CHAPTER ELEVEN

The Paradox of Narcissism

WHILE walking through the local Botanical Gardens recently, a woman wearing a 'Love Yourself' T-shirt jogged past me. T-shirts like that were non-existent in the 1960s, when they all read 'Love' or 'Love One Another'. But preachers of self-love are everywhere today. There are even numerous books extolling the virtues of self-love, including Peter McWilliams's *Love 101: To Love Oneself Is the Beginning of a Lifelong Romance*. The subtitle of that book is actually a tongue-in-cheek comment once made by Oscar Wilde. But it seems that many people have come to take that idea literally.

Today the self-esteem movement is in full swing. As an arm of feel-good culture, this movement has persuaded us that it is not good enough to feel good within ourselves. We must also feel good *about* ourselves. It has grown in force to the extent that it has reshaped childhood education. Teachers in recent years have been trained that a high level of self-esteem is the child's passport to happiness and success in life, as well as to a good education. Less and less emphasis is being paid to self-discipline, hard work, integrity, and helping students gain realistic appraisals of themselves. Instead, young people are being told automatically that they are infinitely talented, phenomenally creative, and erupting with potential in any area that takes their fancy. One zealous school in Alabama went so far as placing banners over all bathroom mirrors that read 'You are now looking at one of the most special people in the whole world.'

Young people find themselves in a culture that tells us to feel good about ourselves regardless of what we are as people. It does not matter if we are spoiled, selfish, indifferent, wasteful, or cruel. We have done our best to make self-esteem unconditional. But many education theorists are now conceding that the self-esteem extravaganza is proving to be a dismal failure in terms of education and personality development.

For instance, it was once thought that high self-esteem was crucial for effective leadership, social skills, and cooperation. The same was said about the ability to resist risky, anti-social, and self-destructive behaviours such as drug taking, smoking, drinking, and unsafe sex. But in all the cases, high self-esteem offers no advantages. In fact, research shows that high self-esteem increases people's likelihood to experiment and to take chances, which can make them more vulnerable to certain problems.

Once considered to be essential for advanced social skills and interpersonal effectiveness, high self-esteem has been shown to give no additional edge in these areas as well. It can even impair social judgement and conscience development. Recent research has found that 'self-enhancers' with highly favourable views of themselves were more prone to acts of aggression such as bullying. They were also more inclined toward irritating behaviour patterns such as bragging, being overly opinionated, and interrupting others in conversation.

Those with high self-esteem appear to have their trumped-up pride hurt more easily, which can trigger in them hostility and other reactions that turn people off. High self-esteem individuals find themselves even more alienated from others when they are not able to conceal their elevated perception of themselves. While high self-esteem leads people to perceive themselves to be more popular and socially adept than other people, this does not correspond to reality when others are asked to rate them. While it is still promoted as a happiness helper, it has become clear that high self-esteem is not all that it was once cracked up to be.

Happiness Key
The wisdom of the world consists in making oneself very little.

— ROBERT LOUIS STEVENSON

Author Robert Louis Stevenson revealed this insight in an 1879 letter to his father. He had finally mastered the irony that life feels better when you look up at it, rather than down on it. The notion that we are not worthy of being happy unless we are big, and full of ourselves, is a thoroughly Western one. Happiness in modern Western culture unfolds in the context of individualism. So it follows that our perceptions of ourselves would be crucial in judging our own degree of happiness. If we are self-satisfied, we are likely to say that we are satisfied with life. This contrasts with collectivist cultures where happiness is tied to cooperation and social harmony, and to being a worthwhile and valued member of the group. In such settings, less effort would be put into self-enhancement, and more into group-enhancement, as a pathway to happiness.

The worst problem comes when self-esteem becomes completely blown out of proportion to the extent that it gives way to narcissism. Unwarranted self-esteem may in many respects be a forerunner of the modern type of 'unwarranted happiness' that has been criticised because it is not founded on anything substantial. In this regard, the type of narcissism and unjustified self-esteem that prevails today is quite interesting in light of the history of the self-esteem movement, which many say was begun by Los Angeles psychotherapist and corporate consultant Dr Nathaniel Branden. While he tried to soften our negative connotations about self-centredness, he was careful to distinguish between healthy and unhealthy types of self-attention. He professed self-esteem that was built on the recognition of the need for love, healthy relationships, and spiritual awareness that he called 'soulfulness'. Since its origins, the self-esteem movement has given way to unbridled me-ism that lacks much scope for a meaningful shared happiness.

The ego has become so artificially inflated in today's cultural climate that the idea of being famous is seen as a requirement for happiness. Local fame is no longer enough. Fame seekers want the whole world as their audience, which may in part be a reaction to the absence of true carers in their local environments. If nobody around me cares, maybe I can get the whole world to care. As our need for affection has been relocated to the public sphere, wooing the mass media has become a popular form of courtship. Ignored people of every description are coming out of the woodwork to set world records or be the first to unicycle blindfolded across the Utah salt flats or leapfrog a thousand beer barrels in less than fifteen minutes.

The familiar cry 'Look at me!' of the neglected child begging for parental attention has spread across the entire Western world as people have become increasingly invisible. For many, fame is imagined to be the only touch that can soothe their gnawing separation anxiety. The problem from a happiness standpoint is that there are very few winners in the fame game. As desperate as we are to be seen and recognised, getting anonymous fans is no easy task. Yet the quest for fame has become inseparable from the quest for happiness.

This trend is eating away at people's prospects for happiness by way of condemning them to almost certain disappointment. They become slaves to a public that is largely a fiction propagated by Hollywood-style hype. The lucky few who make it into the limelight often fall prey to their anxieties about the fickleness of their unknown worshippers, not to mention the loss of privacy and the relationship breakdowns that are part of the package. Despite this, the desire for public fame grows more powerful as our local worlds continue to weaken as a source of recognition. Mixed in with our own ambitions for fame is a trend to bow down further and further to those who have already become famous.

Consumer culture has a large investment in narcissism, just as it does with fame. A lot has been said about today's culture of narcissism, but almost always from a negative point of view. The upside of narcissism is that it is always associated with a high degree of entitlement that sways people to think that they deserve to have things – lots of things. The advertising industry is geared toward selling on the back of rising narcissism. Some of it is blatant, such as commercials that blurt out various messages to the effect '. . . because you deserve it'. Others are subtler at selling things as part of people's growing desire to romance themselves. As narcissism becomes a dominant personality trait, the person gradually becomes shallower and loses the ability to feel deeply for other people. This too increases consumption potential by making people more accepting of the fictionalised world of objects.

The perfect psychological incubator for narcissism is a combination of overindulgence and neglect, which is the story for so many people growing up under modern cultural conditions. It is also the classic condition for the emergence of sociopaths whose main attribute is an absence of social conscience. Narcissists, like sociopaths, experience little guilt, or sense of sin. But sin is not good for the economy. As the cult of the individual has gradually made narcissism acceptable, the sense of sin has been overtaken by the feeling that one has the right to do whatever it takes to satisfy oneself and to feel good.

The sins that remain in our culture of narcissism are largely sins against oneself. We feel that we have done something wrong if we have not gotten the most for ourselves, done the most, or made the most of our opportunities. Other than that, the old-fashioned sins that stemmed from offending others or God are virtually obsolete. The worst sin today is to deprive oneself, which once again is music to the ears of a consumer economy. While feelings of being a sinful person can tarnish happiness, the wholesale erasure of social responsibility can be even more destructive to one's prospects for happiness.

An unceasing preoccupation with personal happiness is in many ways an expression of narcissism. Or at least this is the case with a large percentage of happiness seekers who are looking for happiness by way of what they can draw toward themselves, rather than what they can share with others. Jean-Jacques Rousseau once alluded to narcissism in saying that 'man's nature is not fully mature until it becomes social'. One could say the same thing about happiness; that is, happiness is not fully mature until it becomes social.

The myth of Narcissus is a tragic one. Because he will not surrender himself, Narcissus blows his chances with the beautiful nymph Echo, only to be cursed by an unrelenting self-devotion that robs him of his vigour and beauty. His beloved self never returns his affections, and finally he pines to death, leaving in his place only a lonely flower to preserve his memory. Fittingly, the tale lacks a happy ending. Yet it could be argued that narcissism is not a bad plan of attack. Put yourself first at all times and devote your full energies to feeling good. But narcissism has little to offer by way of happiness, or even self-love. Societies that generate narcissism among their members are dysfunctional ones that have lost sight of the reciprocal nature of human happiness.

The unofficial labels 'middle-class narcissism' and 'normal narcissism' have been used to describe the garden variety of narcissism that is generated by modern consumer culture, which has removed all taboos on selfishness in order to stimulate consumption. As a personality structure, collective narcissism has some advantages since it allows people in a hyper-competitive environment to exploit others without guilt. At the same time, it promotes a low tolerance for frustration that destroys relationships. People often end up fluctuating between expressions of hostility and ungainly attempts to get the approval of others.

Happiness Key

I don't know what your destiny will be, but one thing
I do know: the only ones among you who will be
really happy are those who have sought and found
how to serve.

— Albert Schweitzer

The great theologian and philanthropist Albert Schweitzer understood that service to others is an essential aspect of heart-felt happiness. To sacrifice oneself in the service of others has the paradoxical effect of returning more than one gives. This seems to be one of the universal truths about happiness. Of the richness that comes from serving others, the well-known US Army General Peyton Conway March once commented 'There is a wonderful mythical law of nature that the three things we crave most in life – happiness, freedom, and peace of mind – are always attained by giving them to someone else.' Sadly, the joy of being our brother's keeper is being lost under the reign of narcissism.

Narcissism's harmful effects on the quality of social life are a main reason why narcissism is usually seen as a major obstacle to happiness. There is plenty of evidence indicating that people's interest in the wider social world has been declining as culture has funnelled values in the direction of self-interested materialism. This has revealed itself in various ways. The number of people taking part in most types of social organisations and volunteer services has dropped dramatically in recent decades. Activities that involve group participation are being steadily replaced by ones that people do on their own. Time spent with friends has decreased as people give top priority to their personal ambitions and longings. The tension that is generated when two narcissists try living together is being reflected in the peculiar trend for married couples to live apart from one another. This practice of 'separate togetherness' is becoming for many modern couples the best solution for staying together.

While narcissists are not generally conscious of anything being wrong with their self-centred orientations, there is truth in the point made by nineteenth-century artist and social critic John Ruskin: 'When a man is wrapped up in himself, he makes a pretty small package.' While today's small packages are handcuffed to themselves, they are nonetheless free to seize all opportunities without the burden of deep social commitments. But it is hard for them to escape completely the vacuum in which they operate. It is an unfulfilling experience that sets the stage for rage and eventual despair.

In the absence of social and spiritual ways to define themselves, narcissists often try to compensate by way of pleasures, possessions, and extravagances. This often becomes their masterplan for happiness. But it proves ineffective. Pleasures, for instance, are notoriously short-lived in their ability to sustain positive emotion. Once they are acted upon and consumed, they come to an abrupt end that leaves the person once again feeling empty and alone. If the person persists at attacking sources of pleasure that have dried up, it can quickly become compulsive and addictive. At that point, the individual is left with nothing of consequence to fill their void.

Ultimately, narcissism is all about loneliness, another unpleasant emotion that shadows the modern person as they try to woo themselves into a type of happiness that is far too autistic to be life supporting. Happiness is almost impossible if one is unable to escape the prison of self-interest. The way in which people have shifted their affection to the world of things is an attempt to buy some freedom from the loneliness that haunts their solitary existences.

Sometimes the term egoism is used instead of narcissism to describe the self-inflation that is often a stumbling block to happiness. When it comes to ego, size does matter. Consumer culture loves bloated egos. The bigger, the better. Again this is because it programmes the person to feel entitled to the bonanza of goods that are spread out before us. But shallowness is the end result of approaching one's needs in egoistic ways. In turn, shallow people are destined to a shallow happiness.

In the West, we have lost almost entirely the importance of 'depth' as a source of happiness. But other cultural traditions have framed happiness to a large extent as the fruit of 'deepness'. We do not even have a suitable word to convey a state of depth that delivers bliss. The closest we come is the word 'wisdom', but that does not capture the exhilaration that can spring from depth. We have no counterpart for the Eastern notion of enlightenment that is seen as the fountain from which all true happiness springs.

Living one's life in order to become deep is a legitimate alternative to one focused on becoming happy, especially when people are programmed toward a fragile surface-level happiness. Among the depth traits that have been singled out as rich sources of positive emotion are egolessness, humility, compassion, and the ability to feel and share love.

The value that we place on 'being somebody' is so high that we usually find it quaint to hear of philosophies that portray the ego as a drag on happiness. But even in a society that is stimulated by members who are their own adoring fans, big egos can be cumbersome beasts that cause more pain than joy.

Happiness Key
The sage leaves no footprints when he passes
through the village.

– CHINESE PROVERB

The message expressed in this proverb could not be more opposite to the Western view that we will be happier if we can put our stamp on the world. Unlike the sage, we have become like human graffiti in constant search of empty walls. We dig in our heels and try desperately to make a permanent impression, and even to establish a sort of immortality through this-world accomplishments. But the folly of this approach lies within the truth of our impermanence.

Achieving an understanding of our impermanence actually frees us to experience the sacredness of life. To feed the fantasy that we can leave permanent footprints in the sands of time is to engage in a destructive form of denial that does not yield happiness. By living in such a way that we leave no footprints, we detour from the ego-driven need to form attachments that are not meaningful. We avoid trying to stake claims that do not exist in reality. We also rid ourselves of the impulse to sink our teeth into happiness, which we often see as a pie from which we must get a hefty slice before we can claim victory in life.

According to Tibetan Buddhism, learning the value of egolessness is crucial to inner happiness since it provides tools such as the ability to hear and listen, to reflect and contemplate, and to awaken to 'the obvious'. Its spiritual practices include the 'Dance of the Golden Liberation' that displays symbolically the quest for 'pure vision' that is achieved by the death of the ego. This belief system views the ego as an identity that is made ignorant by way of self-deceptions about oneself and the world. In the Tibetan language, the term for ego is 'dak dzin' which translates into 'grasping to a self'.

The Western mind associates egolessness with ineffectiveness and loss. But in Eastern thought it is seen as a gain that offers sensual delight, freshness, and openness. In *When Things Fall Apart*, the American Buddhist nun Pema Chodron outlines the three basic truths of existence, namely, egolessness, suffering, and impermanence. She describes egolessness as 'a state of mind that has complete confidence in the sacredness of the world. It is unconditional well-being, unconditional joy that includes all the qualities of our experience. In egolessness, wakefulness naturally radiates out when we're not so concerned with ourselves'. By contrast to a joyous state of wakefulness, ego-bound individuals are like muscle-bound ones who give up emotional flexibility in exchange for the illusion of power and control.

Spiritual leader Meher Baba felt passionately that the ego decays values and adulterates happiness. He saw language as a vehicle by which the ego debases one's priorities, which led him to give up speaking when he was twenty-five years old until the time of his death. Baba realised that the ego has an unhealthy way of making us see things backwards: 'It is characteristic of the ego that it takes all that is unimportant as important, and all that is important as unimportant.' It transfers meaning to the meaningless, and peels away meaning from those realms that are rich sources of fulfilment for our human needs.

One of my favourite poems is by the late American poet Cid Corman whose minimalistic style reflects a strong Eastern influence. I attended a poetry reading by him at the University of Wisconsin in 1970, the year of the publication of his book *Livingdying* in which the poem appears. Corman introduced this particular poem with considerable drama, saying it had eluded him for a long time, but that it finally came to him in the middle of a night. With such a big build-up no one was expecting that the poem would be only six words in length. I will include it as a happiness key since I feel it communicates an attitude that can defuse much of the grief that arises from taking ourselves too seriously.

Happiness Key

> A rock stands,
> Where I kneel

— CID CORMAN

What Cid Corman has done with this tiny handful of words – which should be tiny in keeping with the theme – is to create a perfect metaphor for the most profound state of egolessness. It is one in which the person is kneeling, which is a position of reverence, before the lowest of all earthly inhabitants, namely a rock. But even this rock is above him, standing, and worthy of his adoration. Happiness is everywhere from that lowly vantage point. Egolessness has the unexpected effect of opening windows to happiness that remain tightly sealed when the ego looms large.

CHAPTER TWELVE

Lost in the Mirror

WE live in an age of one-upmanship. Standing atop others feels good. We are not quite sure why the upping of others is supposed to make us happier, but we do it nonetheless. Exhibitionism has found its way into our basic beliefs about happiness, and how to approach the world. Humility has lost all credibility as a vehicle to happiness. And it probably is not the best attribute for the type of happiness that is sought today.

Humility is the ability to see through the mirror, and not to be continually distracted by one's own reflection. It has nothing to do with humiliation. The actual word 'humble' traces to the Latin word *humilus*, related to humus or earth. Humility is a state of groundedness in which we are aware that we are part of a larger whole. It prevents the lapses into arrogance that generate conflict and obscure the harmonies that lace themselves into earthly existence. Humility makes it easier to be honest and authentic, which promotes healthy relationships and greater overall social well-being.

Happiness Key

O Snail
Climb Mt. Fuji
But slowly, slowly!!

— Kobayashi Issa

This poem by Issa, the eighteenth-century Japanese poet, is one of the finest examples of Haiku poetry, a literary tradition dating back several centuries in Japan. As with most Haiku poems, which have a maximum of three lines, the theme is subtle and intended to communicate emotion rather than ideas. This particular poem speaks of the jubilance one can experience upon achieving the degree of humility that lets one see the essential equality of all living things. In turn, this fosters the reverence for life that is so vital to an appreciation of beauty, even in the smallest of creatures and events. Here the snail is portrayed as climbing a mountain, which a snail could do in time. What makes this an even greater cause for joy is that the snail is doing it slowly, which means that the snail is being true to its nature.

Despite its ability to contribute to a deep happiness, humility has become largely extinct as a character trait. But at various times in the past, and in other cultures, it was seen as a sign of greatness. Humility is an intelligent self-respect that allows us to maintain a balanced perception of ourselves and the world around us. Within it is a comforting realism that insulates us from false hope, disappointment, and dejection.

Humility is a high level of consciousness that readies the mind for life's ups and downs. It can smooth the transitions from one stage of life to another. Humility stimulates the positive type of small-mindedness that is currently in such short supply. The tremendous turmoil that many people endure by the mere process of aging is due in part to a failure to develop sufficient humility. This speaks of the importance of practising humility on a regular basis, which is a standard recommendation among Eastern philosophers who equate happiness with enlightenment.

As a path to happiness, humility also promotes compassion, another character trait that has been largely extinguished by the culture of narcissism. Genuine compassion is the worst of all poisons for the type of economic institutions that we see today. The current ethos of 'economic rationalisation' is basically about ruthless self-survival and discouragement of anything that might dampen profits or give potential competitors any advantage. This has spilled over into everyday consciousness in which people have come to view themselves as their own charity cases.

The word 'compassion' comes from the Latin words *com* and *passio* which together literally mean 'with suffering'. It may be that the alleviation of others' suffering is a life meaning that transcends all others. But that involves too much compromise for most palates today. Compassion still feels good in small doses, and token acts of charity have even become fashionable, especially if they have an audience. But compassion fatigue sets in very quickly with today's pain-allergic consumers.

Compassion and narcissism are opposite ends of a continuum. Just as self-absorbed narcissists make excellent consumers, highly compassionate people are flops in the consumption stakes. By its design, compassion is a mindscape that makes people and life, rather than objects and pleasures, into top priorities. The whole goal of consumer indoctrination is to shift priorities to the material realm, while sweeping life considerations under the carpet.

It is well known that compassion has been declining rapidly in the past few decades. Today, one comes off as naïve or suspiciously righteous for making compassion into a primary life focus. If not that, the compassionate person is seen as foolhardy for wasting time in a domain that will not hoist one up the ladder of success and financial security. Even people who feel naturally inclined to make compassion a central part of their lives usually override this tendency out of fear. The guilt they sometimes feel by way of turning their back on others is not enough to change their impression that compassion is just too dangerous in a world where one survives by wheeling and dealing.

Those who are concerned about the collapse of compassion see it as a destructive trend that can diminish happiness, loosen the entire fabric of society, and create even larger social injustices than those that already exist. The opening line of William Eckhardt's book *Compassion: Toward a Science of Value* is 'The world is dying from lack of compassion'. The shortage of it is killing us in seen and unseen ways – pollution, poverty, prejudice, violence, overpopulation, and war. As this radical form of faith dwindles, we lose sight of valuable routes to happiness that lie within the all-important value of equality. Compassion ignites an aspect of our basic humanity that can take one to the most meaningful type of success that lies in the offering of oneself.

Happiness Key

If you want others to be happy, practise compassion.
If you want to be happy, practise compassion.

– THE DALAI LAMA

In those words, the Dalai Lama echoes the teachings of a number of Eastern philosophies that regard compassion as a powerful attribute that is indispensable to human happiness. Compassion transcends pity and sympathy. It involves an empathy that lets one truly understand what it is like to see the world through someone else's eyes. Compassionate individuals preserve sufficient time and space in their lives in order to translate their compassion into action, rather than merely voicing it from time to time. Compassion is the knowledge that my own happiness is impossible without your happiness. It is a quality of reward that is unachievable while fixated on our own well-being.

It is heartening to see that a few psychologists are trying to reacquaint us with the fruits of compassion. For example, Lorne Ladner's book *The Lost Art of Compassion* draws on Buddhist traditions in spelling out the value of compassion to mental health and happiness. He writes that 'cultivating compassion is the single most effective way to make oneself psychologically healthy, happy, and joyful. It is a direct antidote to prejudice and aggression'. This is quite similar to something that Eric Hoffer once said: 'Compassion is the antitoxin of the soul: where there is compassion even the most poisonous impulses remain relatively harmless.'

Lives can be transformed in a positive way through the discovery of compassion and its curative powers. As people learn to reach out and operate constructively in a realm that exceeds their own boundaries, there can even develop a sense of being born again, and of having a much greater sense of aliveness. It is far superior to the experience of being encased within oneself. So much of happiness comes from having a heart.

In the modern age, we live on the precipice of unaliveness and will do almost anything to avoid the nothingness that is never far away. Feelings of deadness are one of the most prominent aspects of the narcissistic approach to life. Mental health professionals now speak of the epidemic of 'psychic deadness' that has surfaced under our current cultural conditions. It is usually experienced as boredom, which is becoming the dominant disease facing the Western world. It is an insidious social trend that was recently ranked as one of the 'five principal possibilities of world destruction'. It has been cited as the eighth leading cause of death in the United States. Boredom denies one the ability to feel anything, including happiness.

Chronic boredom is unique to Western culture. Little if any boredom can be found in traditional societies that have an abundance of shared activities, person-to-person communication, extended family interaction, community participation, and other social and spiritual endeavours that provide stimulation and meaning. Even people living in extremely stark environments, like the desert Bedouins, show no signs of the boredom that festers in modern consumer culture.

One American survey taken in 1952 found that boredom was a 'great problem' for 26 per cent of people. When repeated in 1978, the percentage had risen to 38 per cent. Today it is hard to find anyone who does not regard boredom as a serious challenge. It has even infiltrated into the bedroom. The heading for a recent newspaper advice column read 'My Man Falls Asleep During Sex.' One study found that 31 per cent of women and 23 per cent of men were 'completely bored' with sex. In another study that found 43 per cent of women and 31 per cent of men to have 'no interest in sex', boredom was rated as the leading cause. Much discussion was generated by a large-scale Australian survey in 2005 that found that 50 per cent of women had lost all interest in sex. Overwork and boredom were primary causes. Now that sex is largely deregulated and available in endless guilt-free varieties, one might assume that people are reaping the emotional benefits. But as a contributor to happiness, sex is rapidly losing its potency. And rather than helping, the ongoing normalisation of kinkiness and perversion is only hastening its demise.

Boredom attacks the foundations of happiness from several fronts. Research shows that high levels of boredom are toxic to spiritual and existential well-being, and stunt the ability to perceive purpose in life. It has been implicated in a host of social ills, including drug and alcohol abuse, gambling, obesity, addictions, extreme risk-taking, marital infidelity, internet compulsions, vandalism and other 'crimes of boredom', and the relentless shortening of the attention span. Americans now switch television channels, on average, once every three minutes and forty-two seconds. No amount of mental junk food can stop the itch, and eventually anger kicks in. The rising number of 'thrill killings' and 'fun torchings' can often be traced to soul-destroying boredom. When people get to this stage, their boredom has become so profound that they feel almost nothing at all. In many ways they are dead.

Social historians refer to boredom as an eighteenth-century invention that has gradually become the collective condition that is eating up a large part of the human experience. Once praised as the 'dream bird' that propels innovation and the advancement of civilisation, boredom is now generally seen as the crippling ailment of our time. It engulfs us in a restlessness that leads nowhere except to desperation and unhappiness. If boredom was mostly non-existent prior to the eighteenth century, it was because no one had expectations that everything, from breakfast to bedtime, should be a jolt to the senses. Today, thanks to toilet ducks, bubbly flush, and the scintillating prospect of a triple-layered heaven-soft finale, even a visit to the porcelain throne has been injected with the promise of a rip-roaring joyride.

As we came to believe in the fantasy that even the ordinary life could be an unending series of buzzes and novelties, we fell prey to a deadly power that 'makes all things and other human beings and myself fuse into a colourless indifference', which is how twentieth-century philosopher Martin Heidegger described modern boredom. The term 'boredom stress' has emerged as the new psychological weight that has been added to the shoulders of people today.

Leading boredom researcher Alan Caruba, who runs an institute devoted to the study of this problem, describes boredom as one of our main destroyers of happiness. But he explains that boredom often goes undetected because it is everywhere today. In his essay 'Dying of Boredom in America', he writes that 'it's like the air we breathe. It is everywhere in advertising, entertainment, education, politics, and the news.' We live, he adds, in a culture that is determined to help people avoid a single moment of boredom, while at the same time spewing out endless quantities of mental garbage that could bore anyone to death. These include brainless television programmes, stupid magazines, trance-inducing computer games, education that resembles donut making, idiotic fads, simpleton art, and unlistenable music. If you are not bored with consumer culture, something is wrong. But finding one's way out of it is not easy.

One thing we often underestimate is how incredibly boring a narrowly defined consumeristic life can be. It lacks most of the key types of engagement with the world that let people grow out of their own skins. The most malignant strains of boredom are bred by the lifestyles found at the higher rungs of the socio-economic ladder. When interviewed as part of a study of 'suburban boredom', one high-school senior from a posh suburb said 'It's Happyville USA that's doing it. This is the most boring place I've ever lived. There is nothing to do.' It is interesting that the architects and city planners who have joined the discussion about happiness are in general agreement that traditional communities offer much greater prospects for human happiness than the living arrangements that have been born from urban sprawl. Some are predicting an eventual mass exodus from the thousands of Happyvilles that are kindling alienation and killing people with boredom.

Happiness Key

We act as though comfort and luxury were the chief requirements in life, when all we need to make us really happy is something to be enthusiastic about.

— REVEREND CHARLES KINGSLEY

The nineteenth-century minister and poet Charles Kingsley knew that enthusiasm is often all we need to bring us happiness. But enthusiasm is rarely seen on the modern landscape. Instead, ennui is everywhere. A cloud of weariness hangs over people and strips them of passion. Children as young as eight years old can be heard uttering that horribly sad phrase 'Been there, done that.' People are dying to feel alive.

Excitement has become such a rare commodity that people will risk their lives for even a small dose of it. Extreme sports are one of various 'normal' tactics being used for a fix to feel alive.

Very few extreme sports people are aware of the reasons why they tempt fate in such a brazen fashion. I saw an interview with one person whose method of thrill was to scale sheer rock faces without safety equipment. His explanation of why he did it was: 'People set their own limits. If you set no limits, you will be a success.' Some have even described a rush of 'extreme happiness' that is like a turbo-charged spiritual high. But there is the dreaded day of reckoning in which they reach the end of the road, when there is nothing, no matter how extreme, that can compete with their underlying boredom. At that point, no matter how hard they try, they still end up with the maddening sense that they are living out yesterday's news.

Happiness Key

It was the best place to be, thought Wilbur, this warm delicious cellar, with the garrulous geese, the changing seasons, the heat of the sun, the passage of swallows, the nearness of rats, the sameness of sheep, the love of spiders, the smell of manure, and the glory of everything.

– E. B. WHITE

The above passage from E. B. White's classic children's book *Charlotte's Web* never ceases to warm the heart. Through lovable Wilbur the Pig, White was stating the exact state of mind that maximises happiness by keeping everything rare and perfect. Wilbur's world is so delicious because everything is alive, and Wilbur is alive to everything.

E. B. White was very interested in the topic of happiness. He saw the tragedy of people feeling compelled to search further and further from home in order to find happiness. In his 1938 essay 'Removal', he writes: 'When I was a child people simply looked about them and were moderately happy; today they peer beyond the seven seas, bury themselves waist deep in tidings, and by and large what they see and hear makes them utterly sad.' He also once made a similar point while using television as an example of something that rests on the dubious theory that whatever happens anywhere should be seen and sensed by everyone. This approach to the world, he said, has the effect of stripping away the 'rarity value' of the ordinary everyday world, thus leaving people 'specially interested in almost nothing'.

But the modern economy loves nothing more than a society of people trying to spend their way out of the black hole of boredom and ennui. Of this, anthropologist Gregory Bateson wrote recently that 'our economy has become very dependent on the whole cycle of boredom, novelty, more boredom, and more entertainment'. Similarly, James Fitchett of the University of Nottingham presented a conference paper titled 'The Anatomy of Apathy: Perspectives on Consumer Boredom' in which he points out that:

> Boredom has become the chosen pathology of the consumption oriented, market structured age in which we live. It is clear that the preferred citizen has become one whose attempts to be happy have been channelled into escaping the 'Hell of the Same', as it has been called. The booming 'boredom industry' is doing everything in its power to sell the idea that we deserve to be thrilled every moment of our lives.

It is generally assumed that the best way to conquer boredom is to find something that is stimulating. But this approach has proven ineffective with the chronic boredom that is now so prevalent. Stimulation and diversion only seem to hasten the process whereby the bored person reaches the point of no return and becomes unresponsive, and even neurologically drained. Boredom experts have come to see that the best cure for boredom is boredom. It is far better to ride out one's feelings of boredom than to fight them whenever they arise. This breaks the cycle of needing increasingly stronger stimulation in order to get the same relief. At the same time it gradually allows one to reverse the cycle and begin to experience emotion without all the forced promptings.

If you have ever visited Disneyland, you may have been surprised at the huge amount of yawning going on there. It may be the happiest place on Earth for the first half-hour, but from that point on it is a battleground against boredom and stimulus overload. A kinder place to take your children for their emotional development is a place where they will be required to draw on their natural observation skills in order to deal with the subtlety and nuance of that environment.

The desert is a perfect metaphor for the workings of happiness. It is so beautiful and moving because the plainness of its background provides the contrast for the small treasures that punctuate its sameness. Far from being a cause for boredom, this sameness is what accentuates the shades of difference that keep one's emotions alive. Life resembles more closely an exquisite desert than a raucous Disneyland. The desert is an ideal training ground for happiness.

Happiness Key

A certain power of enduring boredom is essential to
a happy life.

— Bertrand Russell

Bertrand Russell wrote that all parents are obliged to help their children acquire the capacity to tolerate boredom. It helps prepare them for the basic life reality that most days are similar to one another and that life's rhythms are slow. It is vital that we stay awake to the small and slow changes that punctuate our day. Being bored is an art that, when performed gracefully and in harmony with the natural flows of life, becomes a gateway for happiness.

The way in which we constantly try to keep ourselves stimulated places an oppressive burden on us, and programmes us to dullness. Eventually the emotions shut down. In Russell's words: 'A person accustomed to too much excitement is like a person with a morbid craving for pepper, who comes at last to be unable even to taste a quantity of pepper which would cause anyone else to choke.' If left to their own devices, people will draw on their own methods for dealing with boredom, and be better off for it in the long run. It encourages them to think for themselves and to develop fresh inner resources. We do ourselves a great favour by accepting that normal boredom is a sign of life. Trying to consume our way out of it is the worst of all solutions. Consumption itself is a passive and uninspired act that invites chronic boredom.

CHAPTER THIRTEEN

The Failure of Success

IN the same way as happiness, we now hear all the time that success is simply a choice. Bookshelves bulge with titles such as *Choose Success*, *Success Is a Choice*, and *Choose Your Personal Success Strategies*. 'The problem with winning the rat race is you're still a rat,' once quipped comedian Lily Tomlin. But the more serious problem is that the rat race has no finish line. A large proportion of today's successful 'rats' are developing what is now being called 'toxic success syndrome'. This trend illustrates how damaging success can be to the quality of one's life.

It is hard to think about success in ways that are not positive. Success and happiness have nearly come to mean the same thing. When people announce that their goal is to be happy, they are likely to phrase it 'happy and successful'. Therefore, when one says that a person is successful, it usually implies that the individual is also happy. But depending on how one defines success, this is not necessarily the case. In fact, mental health workers increasingly are treating cases of pathological success.

Psychologist Arthur Jonathan of Regent's College in London recently wrote an essay titled 'Unhappy Success' in which he detailed the case of a highly successful businesswoman who said at one point in therapy 'You must think it strange that I want to see someone like you when I really have everything in life most people would dream about. I should be happy, but I'm not, and I can't understand why.' In actuality, it is not at all strange that the type of success that this woman enjoyed would bring unhappiness. She is a good example of how success can come at the price of feeling that vital components are absent from life. It can easily corrode happiness by turning life into a one-dimensional exercise in chasing one's own tail.

John O'Neil's book *The Paradox of Success* is a detailed look at how the modern script for success has become a story of life failure for increasing numbers of people. A main reason for this is that 'no limits thinking', along with a steady diet of messages to the effect that 'You can do anything', has caused success to take on mythical proportions. According to O'Neil, mythical success is ruled by various delusions about the actual nature of success.

Among the myths that we have come to believe about success is that it sets you free, when in fact it is more likely to be a Trojan horse. Despite all the surface frills, success often robs people of their time and ensnares them in the very circumstances that are supposed to be liberating. After interviewing many successful business leaders and professional high-flyers, O'Neil observes that 'Some feel that essential parts of themselves are bound and gagged by their commitment to the role that led to their success. When such feelings build up for too long without any release, the result can be a blow-up that tears relationships and careers apart.' Short of that, the person just carries on as a lifelong prisoner of victory.

Another myth is that success is final, and that 'making it' will forever quench our desires. But mythical success is a life orientation that does not culminate in anything except greater ambition and further running along the unending path. Rather than offering happiness or making life easier in an overall way, the winners are never satisfied by any degree of success. They predictably get seduced by additional ways to compound their winnings. Critics of the new success say that, as a society, we urgently need to rethink our current models of success and to define it in more realistic and meaningful ways that allow us to stay connected to others, ourselves, and the planet. As it stands, today's success is often a blueprint for failure.

The word 'success' derives from the Latin *succedere* meaning literally 'to go under'. Since its conception, it has come to mean many things, just as happiness has. The ancient Greek philosophers had little to say about success as an entity in itself. Success tended to be implied by the arrival at an authentic happiness. If one searches through Aristotle's writings, for example, he seems to be describing both happiness and success as the arrival at a level of growth whereby 'the energy of the mind is the essence of life', and in which one's values centre around friendship, dignity, learning, knowledge, truth, excellence, the taming of low-level desire, and the quest for beauty.

Happiness Key

If things do not turn out as we wish, we should wish for them as they turn out.

— ARISTOTLE

Aristotle regarded success or happy living as the unfolding of a consciousness that allowed, in his words, 'the beauty of the soul to shine out'. He once said 'order, symmetry, and limitation; these are the greatest forms of the beautiful'. To keep hammering away for things to be as we want them to be – that is, to continually scramble to make our lives conform to fixed ideas about success – is to forfeit the symmetry needed for a beautiful life.

By its design, the human being is easily tempted by the illusion that life involves getting somewhere or going somewhere. But throughout most of human history, it would have sounded rather crazy to pronounce 'I want to be a success.' At the very least, it would not have made much sense in light of the general belief that one's fortunes were in the hands of higher powers, as well as locked into one's station in life. There is only one reference to success in the Bible, in Joshua 1:8 where God promises Joshua that he will find success if he is obedient, strong, and courageous. When religion was knitted tightly into the fabric of our knowledge, success tended to mean a life that was acceptable to God and other spirit forces. There was little if any notion of 'personal success' of the variety that sees today's rats racing at full throttle.

Another factor that delayed the arrival of toxic success was the way in which people were once too intimately enmeshed with group solidarity and group survival to single out themselves for solo flights of success. In Palaeolithic times, someone whining about not being a success might have been one of those rare occasions when someone did in fact need a club to the head. The need to cooperate cancelled out most prima donna tendencies.

It was not until the Industrial Revolution that significant

numbers of people took seriously the idea of personal success. By the middle of the nineteenth century, the concept of personal success had evolved enough for there to be some demand for advice and guidance. The first how-to-be-successful books were still speaking of social, moral, and religious obligations that were prerequisites to success. But these faded as wider responsibilities were being abandoned in favour of entirely selfish tracks to success. By this time, success had clearly located itself in the realm of material prosperity that was increasingly available to those willing to hop on board the new economic gravy train.

William Mathews's 1874 book *Getting on in the World: Hints on Success in Life* is one of the first self-help success books to warn about the dangerous type of success that could easily prey on people with too strong an allegiance to selfish materialism. He opens his chapter titled 'True and False Success' with a provocative quote by writer G. S. Hillard who had become disenchanted with success: 'I confess that increasing years bring with them an increasing respect for men who do not succeed in life, as those words are commonly used.' Mathews then uses the term 'unsuccessful success' to describe a life that has gained every end, but is a failure as a whole.

Some of Mathews's words sound remarkably modern, such as when he asks 'Shall we subscribe to that dangerous materialism running throughout American life, which preaches that money is the great end and evidence of the possession of intellect, that a man must be a failure unless he culminates in the possession of a check-book.' He seemed well ahead of his time in speaking of the shift from a social world to a 'scrub-race where, at every hazard, though you have to blind the man on your right and trip the one on your left, you must struggle to come out ahead'. In his day, private ambition had already begun to strangle the life out of many people, leading Mathews to say that this always-ascending road was 'too narrow for friendship, too steep for safety, too sharp for repose' – a price so high that we had come to resemble 'a Prometheus chained to the Caucasian rock'. Little did he know over a century ago that he was witnessing a mere dress rehearsal for degrees of ambitious scrub-racing that would cause the road to success to descend from much of our humanity.

Happiness Key
When ambition ends, happiness begins.
– Thomas Merton

Thomas Merton spent many years as a Trappist monk devoted to a life of silence and spiritual contemplation. But in the course of this, he wrote over fifty books, two thousand poems, plus numerous other publications that made him into one of the leading spiritual and literary figures of the twentieth century. To say the least, he was activated. But that is not the same as being ambitious. One can be highly activated and productive without being ambitious. This distinction has been lost as former negative connotations about ambition have been rolled back in order to make more room for greed and gargantuan material aspirations.

We have come to understand ambition as a positive energy that helps individuals to make a success of themselves. In fact, my dictionary defines ambition as 'the determination to achieve success or distinction'. A benign definition such as this makes one wonder why so many great minds of the past slammed ambition as a complete lemon when it came to a vehicle for happiness. Back in the seventeenth century,

Thomas Brooks belittled ambition as a force that slays happiness from many directions: 'Ambition is a gilded misery, a secret poison, a hidden plague, the engineer of deceit, the mother of hypocrisy, the parent of envy, the original of vices, the moth of holiness, the blinder of hearts, turning medicines into maladies, and remedies into diseases.' But bad press like this is hard for us to comprehend today because one crucial aspect of ambition has been erased from its meaning, namely that of excessiveness.

The word for ambition in Middle English was '*ambicioun*' which clearly denoted an excessive clamouring for such ends as wealth, power, or honour. In ancient Greece, the word '*eritheia*' was commonly used to describe ambition, but it again implied excessiveness, as well as selfishness. As we have subtracted the negativity from the meaning of ambition, we find ourselves without a word to identify the blind ambition that is marked by unhealthy overreaching. This type of ambition is so widespread today that it has blended into normality. Yet it causes a great deal of unhappiness as it drives people to lock their sights on extravagant end points that almost guarantee disappointment. A life stretched to the limit with grandiose ambition defies all wisdom about happiness as a way of travel. It can feel like a remedy, but it often turns out to be the disease. Many people are learning the hard way that ambition is an unhappy god. Some of them are experimenting with lifestyles that are lower in ambition and higher in meaning. But blind ambition is being kept alive by the punishing script that has been written for success.

The sweet smell of success had taken on a notable stench by the end of the nineteenth century, even though mass 'success syndromes' had not yet surfaced. This was noticed by William

James, who wrote in a letter to H. G. Wells in 1906 about 'the moral flabbiness of the bitch-goddess SUCCESS. That – with the squalid cash interpretation put on the word success – is our national disease'. He was concerned that success was being seen as the prerequisite for happiness, and that people were losing their own voices and failing to develop unique qualities. In looking around him at the new cash interpretation of success, William James saw a threat to the 'real me' that he realised was 'the particular mental attitude which makes you feel most deeply and vitally alive'.

Much of the literature of the early twentieth century was still portraying success in the context of a social world that had not yet completely unravelled. This was a transition period in which a dissolving social world was allowing success to be defined largely as the effective manipulation of other people. A good example is Dale Carnegie's 1937 classic book *How to Win Friends and Influence People*. It preaches the value of learning techniques of 'handling people' and 'winning them over', and arousing in them an 'eager want', as stepping-stones to personal success and the good life. But Carnegie-style success was still going through the motions of following traditional codes of honesty and integrity. Developing an active interest in the other person was a big part of the picture.

Already in the 1930s there were rumblings that the new free-market model of success was becoming for many people a private religion. In 1930, Bertrand Russell was writing about the trance-like state of the growing ranks of businessmen who were success-driven to the point of sacrificing nearly everything else, except Sunday golf. With success rapidly stirring up religious-like fanaticism and blind following, Russell warned 'If the American businessman is to be made happier, he must first change his religion.' Otherwise, he wrote, the new type of success would only create a poor creature riddled with anxiety, worry, and dimmed concentration.

Russell pinpointed part of the problem in saying 'The root of the trouble springs from too much emphasis upon competitive success as the main source of happiness.' Nearly eight decades ago he was writing about the mounting epidemic of 'nervous fatigue', or what we now sometimes call 'chronic fatigue syndrome'. He too had no way of knowing how much further there was to go in this commercialisation of success.

By the 1980s, the concept of life as a means of profit had exploded into full bloom and the new deity was the 'entrepreneurial spirit'. This particular spirit was unleashed from most social obligations, and tied to things like self-determination, self-devotion, self-discipline, and maximum expenditure of energy. Nearly all of the success gurus were of the motivational 'think big' variety, encouraging unbridled ambition and power tactics designed entirely to get the competitive edge over other people. Getting 'in front of the curve' meant getting in front of others, or even walking over them if necessary. Fuelling this largely anti-social model of success was an unprecedented level of competition that accompanied greed into the centre ring of modern life. Today, competition is the excuse for the type of success that can lack almost all traces of conscience, sometimes even for the successful person's loved ones.

As the social, religious, intellectual, and natural worlds continued to disintegrate, success had nowhere to go except into the value system of the modern age. This meant that people were being condemned to success of the materialistic variety, which became an unending race for an emotional booby prize. As 'unhappy success' became the cultural path to the good life, effort took on a new importance. This had to happen since success had largely become a contest. In times past, a life dominated by work was nothing of which a person would be proud. It was the domain of commoners and low-lifes who had been deprived of free time for leisure, learning, reflection, and relaxation.

The 'work ethic' professed by Martin Luther and John Calvin in the fifteenth and sixteenth centuries blanketed the notion of hard work with positive moral overtones, and kept one out of the devil's workshop. But it was not until recently that work of the self-destructive variety was made into a virtue. Signs of burnout have come to be worn like badges of honour. When people complain that they are being 'run off their feet', they are letting themselves and others know that they are on target. Conspicuous signs of stress are sported proudly, like blood on a warrior's armour, or the musky sweat dripping from a marathon runner – again signs that victory is nigh.

At another level, many people have come to realise that overwork is jeopardising their chances of happiness and well-being. One large-scale study asked about the number of hours per week that people would be happiest to work at the different stages of their lives. Over 57 per cent wanted to work between zero and thirty hours per week at age twenty-five. This went up to 68 per cent for age forty. Despite this, modern notions about success are driving people to increase their working hours far beyond the ideal for a happy and balanced life.

High-speed living has become a vehicle by which to maximise one's productivity and work output. The faster we go, the more we get the feeling that we are racing toward success and happiness. We now live in an age in which the hyperactive 'Type A' personality has become the norm. But psychologists have begun using the term 'hurry sickness' to describe the state of emotional vertigo that stems from the simultaneous juggling of far too many tasks and activities. They point to research showing that the inhuman pace set by hurry-sick individuals can impair memory and concentration. It can also result in worse performance than that seen by people who move along in the slow lane, where some time is reserved for reflection, pondering, and old-fashioned staring out of the window.

Rushed living bypasses most of the exits where happiness and tranquillity are found. But fear keeps people looking for still more ways to accelerate their lives. Self-help books abound on ways to get things done faster. There are books on 'one minute parenting', and 'one minute bedtime stories' to teach parents how to discipline or silence children in the shortest possible time. Lots of people long to slow down, and there is even a 'Slowness Movement' under way. They are aware that their lives suffer from an excess of motivation, and a deficiency of inspiration. Yet the message 'never settle' has been branded into the consciousness of the modern success seeker.

Some can no longer tolerate free time. Personal ambitions are charged and recharged in striving for the pot of fool's happiness that is bestowed upon successful slaves. The term 'leisure anxiety' is being used to describe rat racers who descend into anxiety, and sometimes even panic, when they take a break from work. For some, a vacation is like an act of exposing one's throat to the enemy. People are reaching a point in the quest for unhappy success that they feel comforted by exhaustion in a similar way to which the anorexic is comforted by hunger.

Keeping one's nose to the grindstone has become an increasingly large part of the picture of success. For many, it feels safer to do this. Ruthless forms of competition have raised standards for performance and made perfectionism into a deadly requirement for success. Levels of performance that were once the sole domain of geniuses and virtuosos are now expected of anyone who wants to make it, and especially for those wanting to make it big.

The endless quest for greater productivity is causing levels of workplace stress that are pushing people to their breaking points. The latest phenomenon to come out of this has been called 'desk rage'. One nationwide study in the United States found that 42 per cent of people reported that verbal abuse was a frequent occurrence in their place of work. Nearly 30 per cent admitted that excessive work pressures had caused them to yell at co-workers. About one-fourth of workers said that workplace stress had driven them to tears, while over one-third of them said that this type of stress was responsible for problems such as insomnia, alcohol abuse, smoking, or overeating. Occupational psychologists are predicting that desk rage will skyrocket as productivity takes precedence over people.

Happiness Key

Precisely the least, the softest, lightest, a lizard's rustling, a breath, a flash, a moment – a little makes the way of the best happiness.

– FRIEDRICH NIETZSCHE

These words from Nietzsche's *Thus Spake Zarathustra* touch so beautifully upon the tiny victories and gifts that are superior at offering happiness. But that delicate tapestry gets steam-rolled into oblivion by our indoctrinations to think big when it comes to success. Thinking small has come to feel like a threat. Yet people's commitment to success on a big scale is doing more than causing them unhappiness. Many are failing to cope. In her article 'Addicted to Success', Elizabeth Hartley-Brewer writes that many emotionally spent people are developing unconscious ways by which to trip themselves up so they can opt out of the success game and have an excuse for not chasing the stars.

These 'self-handicapping' measures can include everything from eating disorders, self-harming, hypochondriasis, and depression. Suicide is the most extreme form of opting out. Even the nearly obsolete 'hysterical paralysis' disorders seem to be staging a resurgence as a method of expelling oneself from the game. In Japan, where success demands exceptionally high levels of excellence and uncompromising scholastic dedication, the widespread disorder known as 'hikikomori' has become a serious epidemic affecting 12 per cent of the male teen population, and 6 per cent of the total teen population.

Hikikomori sufferers handicap themselves by locking themselves into their rooms and staying there for months and sometimes years. They often threaten to kill themselves if pressured to rejoin the rat race, which for most of them means the academic rat race. But it is gradually affecting older age groups who are succumbing to the pressures of the hyper-competitive work world. As we would expect, hikikomori is rearing its head in the West as people run out of steam in the chase for unsuccessful success. In 2004, there were over 5000 documented cases in the United States. This is only the tip of the iceberg since this is one of those disorders that is least likely to get reported.

This 'disorder of affluence' now carries the official psychiatric diagnosis of Acute Social Withdrawal. It is limited almost entirely to individuals who come from materially successful families and who themselves have been high achievers at their various endeavours. Jerry Koepp, a director at a Florida-based rehabilitation programme specialising in the treatment of Acute Social Withdrawal, predicts that the prevalence of this disorder is set to explode as growing numbers of people are undone by the inhuman model of success that awaits them today: 'It is a consequence of a social system that has collapsed. As more and more of our young people refuse to assimilate into mainstream culture and reject our core values, the more likely we are to follow in Japan's footsteps.' Koepp says that another contributing factor is that 'American life is terribly boring' and that family life is even worse, filled with unconcerned parents who cannot communicate with their children or refuse to confront them about their apathy.

Yet, despite the misery caused by this and other self-handicapping syndromes, these victims should not be viewed as entirely pathological. Often these self-handicapping syndromes are triggered by the healthy side of the person that realises unconsciously that he or she cannot afford to win by existing rules. While you would not use the word 'happy' to describe any of the victims, many talk about the experience as one of great relief. Sometimes they say that it offers some spiritual exhilaration and a welcome sense of personal safety. At times, they even describe their rooms in terms of a church or cathedral, which again refers to forms of sanctuary from the spectre of success that lurks outside their doors.

The small percentage of celebrated winners in our society is far outweighed by the masses who are worn down by fear of failure and the inner sense that no degree of success is sufficient. But even the winners, writes psychologist Paul Pearsall in his book *Toxic Success*, have come to feel lonely, unfulfilled, and detached from their own success. Many are downright unhappy as a result of the way in which they have attacked success. He spells out how Toxic Success Syndrome has become a scourge that is producing a society of overly geared people who resemble sufferers of ADHD, or Attention Deficit Hyperactivity Disorder. With all their attention focused on the goal of success, they hardly notice that winning costs them dearly in terms of health, relationships, and life enjoyment. Although the new success is ideally suited to consumer economics, it leaves both winners and losers unsettled by 'an eerie vacancy of spirit', as Pearsall calls it.

Tennis great Jimmy Connors once remarked 'I hate to lose more than I like to win.' He is not alone in that sentiment. No sane person enjoys the experience of failure. However, people who sell us on hyper-competition as a model for success have been turning failure itself into a form of winning. Books and videos have appeared in recent years celebrating failure as the path to success. For instance, Charles Manz's book *The Power of Failure* teaches us to recognise that 'failure is the lifeblood of success' and that 'success is the 1% that results from the 99% we call failure'. He sums up the argument for accepting a life revolving around failure in saying 'by wrestling with failure we grow strong wings for soaring to success'. This line of thinking seems logical to seekers who are fully steeped in the notion of success as a contest.

Happiness Key

Naked I was born and naked I am now, I neither win nor lose.

— MIGUEL DE CERVANTES

The real hero of Cervantes's classic book *Don Quixote* is Sancho Panza, the faithful sidekick who tries in his own humble way to persuade Don Quixote of the futility of his repeated attacks on windmills and other imaginary enemies. At numerous points in their ill-fated journey, Sancho recites the above motto about the 'nakedness' that frees him of the burden of winning and losing. Buddha, as we can read in *The Dhammapada*, is teaching the value of this same naked approach to life when he states 'If you give up both victory and defeat, you sleep at night without fear.'

Speaking of sleep, we rarely think of it directly in terms of our potential for happiness. But it is a topic that happiness researchers are focusing on in light of the worsening sleep patterns that have accompanied the quickening rat race. While sleep requirements vary somewhat from person to person, experts say that the ideal amount is around 9 hours per night. This is the average number of hours that people in industrialised nations received back in 1910. By 1975, it had fallen to 7.5 hours, whereas today it is down to 6.9 hours per night and falling.

Sleeplessness has become associated with success. It can even reassure people that they are not wasting time in their scamper for victory. But sleep specialists estimate that 50 million American adults suffer from sleep deprivation to a degree that significantly impairs their mood, mental abilities, energy levels, metabolic functioning, and memory. Research shows that sleep deprivation not only has a general dulling effect on positive emotion, but also promotes feelings of pessimism, anxiety, and irritability. The National Sleep Foundation of America has even blamed a variety of social ills on the epidemic of sleeplessness, including the worsening problem of rage. It certainly takes a toll on happiness, which does not survive long under half-awake conditions.

One of the biggest problems faced by indigenous people trying to adjust to the ways of their European invaders was to somehow come to grips with the concept of being 'on time'. Highly rigid time schedules struck them as unnatural, and as something that could easily jeopardise their collective well-being. We have become so intimate with our clock and watches that we no longer understand the emotional costs of being nailed to the cross of time. A sense of urgency has infiltrated time, and driven us to search out time-saving devices, time management techniques, and anything that will rescue us from the gnawing feeling that there are not enough hours in the day. When all this takes too big a toll on our health and happiness, we are often advised to make more time for ourselves. But this makes people even more anxious since the 'time is money' creed nags them into believing that they cannot afford time. In truth, many people have not left themselves enough time to be happy. They are being too successful.

CHAPTER FOURTEEN

Killing the Things We Love

LOOKING down from Mars, the rat race would look very stupid for so intelligent a species as ourselves. For instance, it would seem most puzzling why we abandon so much happiness for the sake of hyper-competition that leads nowhere except to greater competition. Defenders of competition as a dominant cultural theme are quick to point out its various advantages in terms of innovation, economic growth, and so forth. But as a whole, the type of exaggerated competition that society demands nowadays has far more negative than positive emotional effects. Anxiety is one of the consequences, and we even sometimes refer specifically to 'competition-induced anxiety', and 'competition fatigue'. Over long periods of time, it can interfere with performance, drain morale, and cause a person to neglect social relationships. Rather than basking in the triumphant competition that we sometimes imagine, most people get caught up in the competition trap, which is mostly about losing.

Fear of being a loser in the competition game leads people to abandon most freedoms, and to become unnecessarily enslaved to work at too early an age. They can easily lapse into what is termed Deferred Happiness Syndrome, a mindset in which people postpone the day and tell themselves that long hours of work will translate into happiness at a later point. It defies all wisdom about the actual nature of happiness, and has a detrimental effect on a person's well-being. It is basically a form of self-deception driven by fear.

The trend toward deferred happiness is fuelled in part by the growing aspirations that people have for expensive lifestyles. A high percentage of so-called 'deferrers' feel that they cannot afford all the things they need. Research shows that this is even true of half of the people who make up the wealthiest 20 per cent of the population. But the fact is that the things that people want are getting bigger and bigger, and thus more expensive. It is known as 'supersizing'.

In order to safeguard happiness and health at a time of dangerous resource depletion and environmental crisis, we should be embracing all things small. But from hamburgers to houses, everything is expanding. Over the past five decades, house sizes in the United States have more than doubled, even though family size declined during this same period. The rate of increase has been accelerating even further in the past decade. In Southern California, for example, the size of a new single-family house shot up by nearly 15 per cent between 1996 and 2003. The average-sized new garage in the United States is larger than the typical house of the 1950s. Luxury is also being marketed and bought as if it was essential.

One group of economists calculated recently that, if we were willing to accept the standard of living that existed in 1948, we would only have to work an average of twenty hours per week. The standards of the mid-1970s would let us get away with thirty hours per week at most. But we are working longer and longer hours, despite technological advances that should be allowing people to finally escape captivity.

Happiness Key

The happy have whole days, and those they choose.
The unhappy have but hours, and those they lose.

— COLLEY CIBBER

Colley Cibber was a popular actor and playwright in early eighteenth-century England. He touches here on the happiness that should, it seems, come by way of abundant free time. After all, the Eden for which our species has yearned for 10,000 years is one where whole days are ours for the choosing. Cibber once wrote about the way in which a simple cup of tea can bring great happiness when savoured without the bitter taste of pressured hours: 'Tea! thou soft, sober, sage and venerable liquid; – thou female tongue-running, smile-soothing, heart-opening, wink-tippling cordial, to whose glorious insipidity I owe the happiest moments of my life, let me fall prostrate.' In this way, it seems that so many wonderful little things in life could be savoured, if only we would make the time for them.

Our best chance for a return to the happy and peaceful Eden that legend recalls came in the form of the technological revolution. High technology offered us a cross-road that could have changed the course of everyday life for the human being. It was what we had been waiting for, namely a point of exit from the grind and a liberation of time. In the 1970s, we were still heralding in the young high-tech revolution as an historical event that would do exactly this.

We had visions of a new technological world, full of

re-found freedoms that would awaken society spiritually, intellectually, and socially. But no one any longer even pretends that technology will lift the yoke from our shoulders. Quite the reverse. We went the way of commercialising technology and making it into part of our enlarging package of personal desires. The dream of a partial return to Eden evaporated as technology turned out to be a slavemaster that would reward us with still another social disease, namely 'techno-stress'. Rather than reacquainting us with the ones we love, our commercial love affair with technology took us even further away from them.

Happiness Key

The supreme happiness in life is the conviction that we are loved.

– Victor Hugo

Over the ages, many people have come to the same conclusion as nineteenth-century writer and politician Victor Hugo, who voices these words in *Les Misérables*. To be is to be loved. In turn, the healthiest forms of happiness are experienced and expressed as love. There are not many sources of happiness that cannot be traced to love. By its highest estimation, love completes us, brings us into harmony, gives us meaning, and binds together all the elements of the universe. In its various forms, love is what human beings do with their need for intimacy. Without intimacy, there is no happiness. Failure to find intimacy will drain the happiness and zest out of a person faster than anything.

One reason that the technological revolution failed completely to rescue us from work and return us to our loved ones is that work itself had become a total way of life. Even though modern society was given the key to release the workers to some extent, the workers themselves had nowhere to go. Again, this was because the other domains of life had atrophied. In many ways, modern working beings had forgotten how to love, and how to express themselves spiritually, intellectually, and physically. The mind, the body, the 'other', and God had all become strangers. At heart, people were afraid to abandon their work, and it continues today to take on greater value.

As this happens, workers have come to see the workplace as their psychological home. A number of studies show that an increasing percentage of people would rather be at work than at home with their families. This trend has been encouraged by employers who continue to transform the workplace in a way that keeps their 'zero-drag' workers happy in the face of longer hours and greater demands for productivity. When workers say 'I love my job', they could easily be describing the only love in their life. For many, work has become everything. But it rarely manages to meet their emotional needs in a way that promotes true happiness.

The immortal last lines of Oscar Wilde's poem *The Ballad of Reading Gaol* lament:

> And all men kill the things they love,
> By all let this be heard,
> Some do it with a bitter look,
> Some with a flattering word,
> The Coward with a kiss,
> The brave man with a sword.

To that list we can now add work and success. We now speak of the 'invisible parent'. Between 1960 and 1986, the amount of parental time available to children dropped by ten hours per week. This number has continued to drop, which is why so many modern children lack entirely a 'psychological parent'. Surveys show that over 40 per cent of working people admit that their long hours at work have a detrimental effect on family life. But many turn around and claim that they are being held hostage by financial obligations. Home does not exist in the former sense of the word. In truth, the escalating hours that people are funnelling into work are largely in order to support the false needs that they have adopted. Working for one's family has become a substitute for caring for one's family.

A recent study in Great Britain found that 70 per cent of children aged five to twelve behaved badly. This was blamed on a combination of absentee parents, inconsistent discipline, bad diet, and preoccupation with technology. Making matters worse is the tendency for work-focused parents to force 'quality time' – another convenient myth of the consumer age – onto their children. Typically the parent overindulges the child while neglecting to set any restrictions. It is understandable that the 'dysfunctional family', as it has come to be known, is now the norm.

Also the norm is the 'frantic family', the familiar scenario in which parents and children scurry from one appointment to another, rarely intersecting each other's inner worlds. The home serves as little more than a quick pit-stop in the marathon of modern consumer life. Not everyone is happy with the fact that personal ambition is more powerful than familial love. In fact, increasing numbers of mothers and fathers are suffering from what is known as 'Guilty Parent Syndrome'. Yet usually this guilt is not sufficient to pry them away from their mission of having it all. Many working beings experience their own ambition as their most trustworthy friend. It feels like a lifeline. But emptiness always follows on the heels of one's ambitions when in the process we kill the ones we love.

Happiness Key

Wisdom is oft times nearer when we stoop than
when we soar.

– WILLIAM WORDSWORTH

These words by Wordsworth from *The Excursions: Book III* would be just as true if we replaced the word 'happiness' for 'wisdom'. Either way, the message is that we often end up missing a great deal by shooting for the stars. Setting our sights closer gives one a much better chance of happiness by keeping love as the focal point of our lives.

Love is one of the worst casualties of consumer culture, which finds it difficult to incorporate much genuine love between people into its panacea of work and consumption. By encouraging individualism, narcissism, and materialism, it banishes love to the sidelines. Filling the gap left by love is an increased value on personal happiness, possessions, net worth, and image. Whereas love was once a power to which one had to surrender, now it is a conscious part of one's life portfolio. Even children are no longer expected to get uncompromising love and attention. They too must content themselves with being part of the portfolio.

We live in the era of 'exchange relationships' and 'consumer marriages', both of which have evolved in order to make room for the new brand of happiness and success. Old-style relationships were more communal in the sense that it implied a mutuality and reciprocity. When one person gave to the other, it was seen as a contribution to the overall relationship. The modern exchange relationship, however, involves two participants who are largely self-focused and thus likely to see the union in terms of an economic exchange. An expectation has emerged that there should be a worthwhile return from any investment of energy, time, or finances into the relationship. In the process, the other person has become a disposable part of the portfolio if they are not deemed to be worth it.

The effect this has had on marriages shows up not only in the high rate of divorce, but in the actual factors that trigger divorce. In the past, divorce implied an unhappy marriage. Rising divorce rates were blamed on falling levels of happy marriages. Now, however, being happily married is no longer reason enough to stay together. Around 30 per cent of divorces are of the new 'conflict-free' variety in which one or both partners have the vague sense that life would be better elsewhere. What this really means is that the binding power of love has become so weak that many husbands and wives are ready to break up their marriage because of the inkling that they would be happier by moving on. They do not end up any happier, as research shows, but they nonetheless follow their happiness whims.

Children suffer the most from conflict-free divorces since they struggle with profound confusion about the reasons for their seemingly happy parents' decision to break up their family. Also they are more likely to blame themselves. Previously, even if marriages became conflicted, people put their children first. In 1962, 50 per cent of couples said they would stay together for the sake of their children, whereas the percentage today stands at slightly over 10 per cent. The committed and unconditional love of others is being lost as a source of happiness.

The same fate has befallen friendship as a source of happiness. In reading about the history of friendship, one discovers that in ancient times it was generally regarded with great reverence. Aristotle attached so much value to friendship as a source of meaningful happiness that he acclaimed a friend as a 'second self' who could make us more aware of our own existence. At various times in the past, true friendship was hailed as 'the crown of life' and 'the happiest and the most human of all forms of love'. It has also been called 'the most spiritual of the affections'. In short, friendship was seen as a big part of having a happy and successful life. Friendship was still held in high regard in the sixteenth and seventeenth centuries when it had the added value of being seen as a refuge from political corruption, and religious oppression, as well as a source of relief from inhumane work. A great deal of comfort and enjoyment is added to one's world by having a true kindred spirit – someone who gives us life, and someone we would die for.

Happiness Key

To have joy one must share it. Happiness was
born a twin.

– Lord Byron

Since poet Lord Byron wrote those words in the early eighteenth century, friendship has undergone a huge transformation, with negative implications for happiness. Writing in the 1950s, religious scholar C. S. Lewis was one of the first people to describe the way in which modern friendship had become nothing more than 'something that fills up the chinks in one's time'. It has continued to take a back seat to self-interest and a hectic consumer lifestyle that does not leave much time for getting to know each other.

The strong competitive element of society has changed the

way we look at other people. Trust, sometimes referred to as 'the chicken soup of social life' due to its health-giving effects, has been declining steadily over past decades. In 1960, 58 per cent of people had a sense of 'generalised trust' in other people. In 2003, that had fallen to 34 per cent.

The same has happened to loyalty, another core element of friendship that has become largely extinct. The Roman senator Seneca praised loyalty as 'the holiest virtue in the human heart'. Like trust, it contributes to happiness and well-being in the same way as faith. Loyalty is a willingness to act on, and abide by, one's love. The mere experience of loyalty reinforces one's commitment and acknowledges its strength and importance.

But research shows that loyalty has largely vanished, not only from the realm of friendship, but all other areas of life as well. One recent study titled 'The Decline of a Prized Virtue', by Australian academics Sharyn Rundle-Thiele and Rebekah Bennett, found that only between 6 and 9 per cent of people are 'highly loyal', depending on age group. The exception was the over-fifty-fives who came in at 15 per cent. Zero per cent of eighteen- to twenty-four-year-olds were 'highly loyal', which these researchers blamed on the trend in modern society for people to be more cynical, less trusting, less tolerant of sacrifice, and more interested in instant gratification than in previous eras. They conclude by saying that the younger generation may never know loyalty.

Happiness Key

The highest compact we can make with our fellow is:
Let there be truth between us two forevermore.

– RALPH WALDO EMERSON

Honesty, still another of the nearly extinct character traits, is certainly the ideal basis for any meaningful relationship, as well as a fulfilling type of happiness. In the end, dishonesty always takes more than it gives. But the hunt for happiness now takes place in what Erich Fromm so aptly called 'The Age of the Pleasant Personality'. Increasingly, relationships of all types are being approached in terms of going through the motions and saying the right things. The goal of nice-ism and the charm offensive are to keep others happy, which is seen as part of the new personal success. But it is actually a form of domination.

The decline of authenticity has shown up in the way we communicate to our children, spouses, and friends. It contributes to the vast pool of loneliness that surrounds people's desperate search to connect with one another. Many unattached individuals describe the near impossibility of meeting a sincere human being as the biggest problem in their lives. Never before has it been so difficult to locate sincerity in other people. Gamesmanship and exploitation are so ingrained into us that we fall back on it reflexively when we encounter prospective mates. Forty years ago there was a study at a Midwestern university in the United States comparing the effectiveness of a large number of men's pick-up lines. The one that outperformed all others was 'This makes me a bit nervous, but I'd really like to meet you.' Nowadays, if you read all the complicated advice on how to meet other people by way of cunning and calculation, you quickly see that this sort of simple honesty eludes us as a pathway into new relationships. And when people do meet, it is likely to descend quickly into a measurement exercise of the overall assets and potentialities of the other person. No great cause for optimism came from the 2005 study of pick-up lines by two British psychologists which found the best one to be 'It's hot today, isn't it? It's the best weather when you're training for the marathon.'

Even though people are wedding themselves to dishonesty, they can still detect it in others. This is even true when it comes to the dishonesty that is helping to erode sexual happiness. For instance, research shows that fake orgasms are on the rise, most notably among men. The percentage of men who felt inclined to fake orgasms thirty years ago was negligible. Recent research in England, France, and the United States shows that around one-fourth of men are faking orgasms, even though 75 per cent of women can tell that they are fake. Bedroom boredom undoubtedly contributes to the need to orchestrate an orgasm. But faking it has become acceptable in all spheres of life. We are losing sight of the pleasure that comes from being ourselves, and from being imperfect. The climax is overrated as a source of happiness. So too is perfection.

CHAPTER FIFTEEN
Happy Societies

ONE could start in a number of ways to learn about the geography of happiness. Positive mental health is a big part of happiness. While there is more involved, we are bound to learn something about happiness from looking at the reasons why people in some societies do not suffer from certain mental problems.

There are numerous non-Western societies that are far superior to Western ones when it comes to psychological health. For instance, medical anthropologists have documented a number of societies that are completely free of postnatal depression. The reasons for this have to do with the great value attached to childbirth, as well as the cultural rituals that can take the form of song, poetry, massage, elaborate meals, and sharing in the care of the child. This combines with other active involvements on the part of the community, both before and after the actual birth, that gives the mother a deep sense of emotional support. Often childbirth comes with official recognition of elevated status. It is now generally agreed that postnatal depression is primarily limited to modern Western cultures where it has a prevalence of around 20 per cent for the full-blown disorder, which includes clinical depression, and over 50 per cent for the less severe 'maternity blues'.

Curiously, weddings in the West are also beginning to cause the blues, with researchers now pointing out the rising rates of 'postmarital depression'. They explain it in a similar way to postnatal depression. In both cases, large quantities of fantastic and commercialised expectations are followed by a disturbing sense of one's aloneness and of the indifference of the wider group. By contrast to societies with intact moral nets, the West is overrun with depressed mothers, brides, and grooms.

The mid-life crisis that is a source of unhappiness for many people in modern consumer culture is also absent from most non-Western settings. Traditional cultures usually hold middle age in high regard. They are largely unaffected by the self-loathing that is spawned when cultures degenerate into ones that worship youth. In each case, the mid-life crisis is nowhere to be found. Many non-Western societies also lack the assumption of 'biological decline' that is assumed in the West to diminish happiness as a consequence of normal aging.

It is worrying that the Western mid-life crisis is occurring at increasingly early ages as people bump up against extreme doubts about what they are doing and what they have accomplished. Consumerism's dead end is even being reached by people in their twenties and thirties. Many have fallen into what economists call the 'fulfilment-deficit cycle' in which they can no longer be nourished through the satisfaction of the false needs that have been instilled in them. Even the conscious chase for happiness can help usher in a crisis as people come to feel that life has not been delivering happiness on the scale that they expected, which causes them to question their core life strategies.

While societies that favour positive mental health also tend to favour happiness, it is possible to find exceptions. For years I have been studying and writing about the Kaluli people of New Guinea. They are one of the best known examples of a society that lacks any signs of clinical depression. In thirty-five years of anthropological research, no cases have been documented. They seem to have a cultural blueprint that does not allow for prolonged states of deflated mood. The Kaluli language has no word for depression, sadness, or anything resembling a protracted state of unhappiness. With all that said, the reason that the Kalulis are entirely immune to depression may be the main reason that I would not call theirs an exceptionally happy society.

When cultures are set up for people to express themselves fully across a wide range of emotions, they are much less likely to develop depression. This is because depression is largely the result of the internalisation of emotion. Depression has often been linked specifically to the internalisation of anger, which is why it is often treated with assertiveness training and other therapies that encourage people to vent their feelings. The Kalulis have no problem whatsoever when it comes to anger. Quite the reverse, the expression of anger is the dominant theme of Kaluli culture. Social standing is determined by how dramatically one can display anger. If the gods are not good to them, they even get angry at them and show it through high-energy ceremonies that symbolically attack the offending deities. Weddings even turn into collective displays of anger since this allows people to get revenge for eventual injustices such as the death of a spouse or child.

In short, Kaluli people are able to externalise virtually all negative emotion by way of this culturally approved anger mechanism. Any biological or genetic predispositions toward depression do not stand a chance against this emotional cleansing process. But the price they pay is that this adaptation inevitably creates friction, and channels too many forms of expression in the direction of anger. It works as a highly effective contraceptive for depression, but it is not the best formula for overall happiness and social well-being. To look at them, you would not jump to the conclusion that they are a culture of joy, as is the case with certain other cultures.

The first time I came face to face with a group of people who appeared to be extraordinarily happy was in 1978 when the Tazara train – en route from northern Zambia to Dar es Salaam in Tanzania – broke down in a remote part of the eastern Tanzanian bush. The passengers roamed around for several hours until repairs were made. I wandered toward the edge of the bush where a group of bubbly children were gesturing for me to follow them, which I did. For the next hour, I found myself at a little village where I saw more happiness and life enjoyment than I had ever before witnessed.

Although highly paradoxical in light of their material circumstances, this perception of the happiness of rural Africans tends to be the rule. If you ask any director of an African aid agency, that person will tell you that volunteers come away dumbfounded by the high levels of happiness in the African people. One head of an American aid agency in Kenya commented that it had become a cliché for volunteers to be struck by the zest and jubilance of the Africans and to say in wonderment 'The people are so poor, they have nothing – and yet they have such joy, they seem so happy.'

The Dalai Lama is among the many notable thinkers who commented on the emotional deprivation that emerges from materially abundant societies. In *Ethics for the New Millennium*, he writes:

> Those living in the materially developed countries are in some ways less satisfied, are less happy, and to some extent suffer more than those living in the least developed countries. They are so caught up with the idea of acquiring still more that they make no room for anything else in their lives. As a result, they are constantly tormented and plagued with mental and emotional suffering.

In the last five or so years, there has been a lot of media attention given to scientific happiness research that has sought to rank countries on the basis of their happiness. Most of these have involved paper-and-pencil types of tests in which people were asked to indicate if they were 'very happy', 'quite happy', 'not very happy', or 'not at all happy'. A major shortcoming of going into a society and asking how happy people are is that their answer derives partially from comparing themselves to others around them. Even if the people in the Tanzanian village that I visited were the world record holders for happiness, most of them would in all likelihood say that they were about average. This is despite the possibility that the least happy of them might be happier than the happiest person in a less happy society. Conversely, in a land of happiness lightweights, people are going to gauge their happiness to a considerable degree against other lightweights and again conclude that they are not too far from average.

There is also the issue of the cultural value or taboo placed on happiness itself that will cause people to exaggerate or downplay their self-report of happiness. For instance, unlike Western society where one is proud to be happy, the Ifaluk people of Micronesia frown on those who show happiness since it is believed that happiness can cause people to neglect their social obligations. Yet these and other considerations have not deterred researchers from using simplistic self-report measures in trying to compare happiness between different societies. In fairness, the findings probably end up giving us some information that is a starting point for discussion about cultural influences on happiness.

The World Values Survey gathers happiness data on a periodic basis in a large number of countries. In addition, they obtain information about diverse values and living conditions that give an indication of the general well-being of people in different societies. In one of their recent surveys, sixty-five nations were included. Unfortunately, some of the hot favourites for the happiest country award were not included. One was Thailand, which has a long-standing reputation as a nation of exceptionally happy, smiling people. They have been known for generations as 'The Land of a Thousand Smiles'. My own experiences from Thailand, where I once lived, worked, and even got married, certainly bore out the truth of that label. This was far more apparent in the countryside, although even the unforgiving demands of Bangkok did not erase the smile that came so quickly to the Thai people. Their apparent happiness was a regular topic of discussion among us envious Westerners.

The findings of the World Values Survey have been interpreted in different ways. When self-reports of happiness were looked at in the broader context of such measures as the quality of friendships, marital happiness, and the ability to grow old gracefully and with respect, Nigeria turned out to be the surprising winner. Mexico, Venezuela, El Salvador, and Puerto Rico were not far behind. The Latin American countries in general scored highly, both when happiness ratings were looked at alone or factored in with other indirect measures of well-being and happiness. They also came out at the top in an international study of happiness among university students. In that one, Puerto Rico, Colombia, and Spain headed the list. It is also possible simply to look at the percentage of people who claim to be 'very happy'. In this case, Venezuela came out on top at 55 per cent.

Venezuela is a country that suffers from corruption, internal strife, and a rising poverty rate estimated at 75 per cent. Those who have commented on the puzzlingly high levels of happiness there tend to say that it resides in their ability to enjoy the simple pleasures of health, family, and friends. Their strong ties to religion are also seen as a contributor. One rarely hears about depression and suicide there, and almost no one complains that life is unfair or that their lot in life is lacking. In a recent international survey of sexual happiness, the Venezuelans again topped the list. They are a vibrant, sensual, and fun-loving culture despite all the obstacles that have been thrown in their way.

The hardships that they face have caused Venezuelans to lower their expectations in a way that allows them to approach life with a wider attitude of acceptance and thanksgiving. Ironically, a certain amount of adversity may be useful when it comes to promoting happiness by keeping expectations under control. It is one of the reasons that Venezuelans are so often said to be one of the most contented people in the world. Rising expectations always raise the height to which we must jump in order to be happy and at one with the world.

Guatemala is another Latin American country that has many of the same social structures as Venezuela. Visitors often come away with the impression of Guatemalans, especially rural ones, as exceptionally happy and contented. My nephew, Ben Schumaker, is an avid humanitarian who founded the Memory Project aimed at increasing awareness of the plight of orphaned children in the Third World. He also recently published the book *Astonishing Stories for a Hopeful Humanity* that again draws attention to international humanitarian issues, while encouraging people to work for positive change. The time that Ben spent in rural Guatemala led him to comment on the people in the following way, which helps us understand certain aspects of happiness:

The first thing I noticed is that they are more naturally content with life, and more relaxed. They work every day, but do not get as stressed out about it. They do not walk as fast; they move at their own pace, and do not talk as quickly as Westerners. The rural Guatemalans smile easily at things that Westerners would probably not find enjoyable. In the USA, children seek enjoyment from ultra high-tech video games, zany television shows, and over-stimulation by things like laser tag and adrenalin-pumping extreme sport activities. Children in rural Latin America do not have any of that, and have fun with activities that would bore most American children. They play simple games like tag. I saw three Mayan girls, around nine or ten years old, having the time of their life running around a puddle and splashing into it every once in a while. One might see three American girls doing the same thing, but it would be a departure from the norm, whereas in Latin America it is commonplace. Adults smile and laugh readily just by engaging in conversation, and what strikes me most about adults is that I've never heard them use sarcasm. The humor and happiness seems to be very pure. By contrast, one often hears sarcastic, bitter, and sick humor in America. We have a much higher threshold for pleasure than do the people of rural Latin America. We spend so much on vacations, boats, hot tubs, antique cars, gigantic-sized televisions, etc., in a search to be happy. But they are just as happy, probably happier, without all those privileges. They taught me that our pleasure and happiness thresholds have grown far too high.

Among other things, Ben's description captures the importance of innocence as a shortcut to happiness. One thing that all happy societies have in common is that they retain a certain degree of innocence. Without it, happiness escapes people. Yet the word 'innocence', which actually originates from the Latin meaning 'not to harm', has taken on negative meanings such as ignorance, unawareness, and inexperience. For younger people, it has the added tinge of being uncool, gullible, and sexually immature.

Modern consumer culture cannot bear innocence. It seeks to destroy it and to convert people into unimpressionable bundles of hunger who are willing to prostitute themselves to every product and experience. Ten-year olds can already be seen wearing the persona of an old sea dog, with weary worldliness advertising that they have seen it all, and that nothing is any longer surprising, exciting, or noteworthy. What makes this so tragic is that the death of innocence is also the death of happiness, passion, and a sense of the sublime.

Some have drawn a distinction between 'negative innocence' and 'positive innocence'. The latter of these is born from wisdom about the need to retain the child-like elements in oneself. This becomes the foundation for future happiness. It is so important to cherish all the things one has never done, or knows nothing about. Happiness depends upon retaining a certain amount of virginity.

Happiness Key

To see the World in a Grain of Sand
And a Heaven in a Wild Flower,
Hold Infinity in the palm of your hand
And Eternity in an hour

– WILLIAM BLAKE

It would be hard to improve on those opening lines from Blake's *Auguries of Innocence* in trying to describe a state of mind that is predisposed toward happiness by way of innocence. Further on in the poem, Blake writes that 'We are led to Believe a Lie' and made to forsake the 'infant's faith' that lets us bask in the simple joys that are ours when we become 'a Babe in Eternity'. Elsewhere, Blake wrote about a similar state of innocence that produced people who could 'By mere playing go to heaven.' Those who understand how the death of innocence has damaged our prospects for happiness preach about the need to somehow arrive at a 'second naïvety' that once again lets us experience happiness without the burden of sophistication. But the fear of innocence is too strong for most.

The media had a field day when Nigeria came in as the happiest country. This was due in part to its reputation as a politically unstable and volatile country, which makes it an unlikely candidate for the title of happiest country. But I was not surprised that an African country came out on top. If other African countries had been included in the survey, I am sure that many of them would have done at least as well as Nigeria. I conducted cross-cultural research on religion and mental health in Nigeria, which made me aware of the intensely religious nature of the Nigerians. To whatever extent a spiritual happiness contributes to overall happiness, I had no trouble believing that they would be toward the front of the pack, despite their many adversities.

Their casual relationship to time is another factor that is always mentioned in trying to explain the paradoxical happiness of many African groups. The term 'African time' is sometimes used in condescending ways by those who are ignorant of this aspect of traditional African culture. Such people forget that the high status that we attach to timeliness and the profitable use of time is often at the expense of our social needs. African time runs on a social clock. People take and make time for each other. Also, almost every African society has a saying that means 'no worries', an attitude that is greatly facilitated by the non-threatening nature of time. In a related way, Africans often do not suffer from the modern illusion that individuals are in total control of their lives, or that the world responds at the snap of a finger. Time still mingles with their natural instincts to laugh and enjoy each other's company.

Nosson Slifkin, a rabbi and author of several books, recently wrote a piece titled 'Hakuna Matata' which means 'No Worries' in the language of the Masai people of Kenya. He touches on the concept of African time as he describes his personal experiences in East Africa. He writes that 'the Africans were the happiest, most contented people I have ever seen. They were genuinely happy. Despite being horrifically poor, they were perpetually smiling and singing'.

Slifkin encountered one well-intentioned Westerner who was trying to help these people by getting the local villages connected to the internet. He reacted negatively to this idea, saying 'the people seemed so happy and content; why transform them into Americans – neurotic, depressed, and undergoing therapy?' Slifkin based this opinion on his impressions that the remarkable happiness of the local people was due to the fact that they did not have many means of outside comparison that would make them feel that they were missing out on something, or that life could be better if they had more. Herein lies the quicksand in which one can quickly find oneself when one's happiness is viewed in the light of the ocean of alternatives that could, in theory at least, lead to more happiness. It is a great bonus from a happiness standpoint to be spared such comparisons, or to be able to see through them.

The Nigerians, like other African people, are well known for their optimism. In January of 2000, an international survey was conducted asking people from various nations the simple question 'Will 2000 be better than 1999?' Nigeria was the country with the highest percentage of 'yes' responses, followed by Venezuela, and Malaysia. In 2003, the same survey was conducted asking if 2003 would be better than 2002. First place went to Kenya, with Nigeria coming in third place. The positive emotion that is generated by their unconquerable optimism does not seem to be tied to economic factors, as it is in European and North American societies. Rather, it seems to be a permanent part of their culture that evolved as an emotional buoy that is available during bad as well as good times. All around Nigeria, one hears 'Ee go better, ee go better', an often-used pidgin English phrase telling each other that things are looking up. With this mindset, it is not difficult to look at the proverbial glass as half full, rather than half empty.

A number of follow-up attempts were made to find out why the Nigerians are so happy. The most common reasons given were God, music, dance, and simplicity of needs. British international affairs writer Jonathan Power wrote an article titled 'Nigeria: Happiest Nation on Earth?' in which he cites some of the specific comments made by Nigerians to explain their happiness. The remark by one woman was quite typical: 'Many of us are happy because we don't ask for much. If God gives us food we easily become happy. We are not greedy.'

A Nigerian businesswoman felt that the Nigerians' strong sense of caring and social responsibility contributed to their bountiful happiness: 'We Nigerians look after each other. If I know you are hungry or ill, I will try and help.' One engineer stressed the religious factor: 'Happiness was in our tribal traditions and religion built itself upon that. Have you ever seen such a religious people? Of course it goes too far in many cases and we become too fatalistic.' Ninety per cent of Nigerians attend church on a regular basis, compared to 40 per cent in the United States, which is one of the most religious Western societies.

Nigeria's Princess Gloria Iweka commented that Nigerians do in fact perceive themselves to be an exceptionally happy society of people. As she put it, 'You see it in how we move. It's a movement inside us and in society. We feel full of music and love of God.' Based on his own experiences and all his interviews with people, Jonathan Power concluded 'I can see all the ifs and buts, and have heard all the caveats, but yes I conclude, Nigeria has tasted happiness, and more than most.' To that I would add that many groups around Africa can teach us some of the mysteries of happiness.

Happiness Key
We should consider every day lost on which we have not danced at least once.

– FRIEDRICH NIETZSCHE

Find me a society of people who dance every day and I will show you a happy society. Dance is a cultural universal that has long ties with human happiness. As Princess Iweka pointed out, happiness has a lot to do with movement. Throughout Africa, especially outside of the cities, you notice immediately how dance-prone everyone seems to be. Children dance on and off throughout the day. But a great many adults will also break into dance at the slightest provocation, even a pun or silly remark. My years in Africa led me to appreciate dance as one of the most effective mechanisms by which room is made for positive emotion. There is even historical evidence that Jesus Christ was no stranger to the miracle of dance, and that he incorporated it into his teachings. As one early Christian mystic in the tradition of St Bernard wrote:

> Jesus the dancers' master is
> A great skill at the dance is his
> He turns to right, he turns to left
> All must follow his teaching deft

In 1983, my wife and I were working on a project aimed at preserving traditional First Nations music. As part of that, we had the honour of being invited to the Six Nations of the Grand River Reserve in Canada in order to record live performances by Iroquois elders Jimmy Sky and Hubert Buck. In speaking with them, we were struck by the degree to which both music and dance had a large historical role to play in the happiness and social well-being of these people. By chance, I recently ran across the transcript of an interview with Jimmy Sky that was conducted by Jim Metzner, the producer of the Pulse of The Planet radio programme (www. pulseplanet.com). It was completed just before Jimmy Sky's death in 2000. In the interview, Jimmy talks about dance as an all-important language by which happiness was communicated and experienced by the Iroquois people. In speaking specifically about social dances, he says 'The role is to show your happiness. Like our singers, it makes them happy to see these people dancing.' Then he goes on to describe the way in which dance was always an inseparable part of life.

> Dancing is just part of us, it's always been there. You can't really say how long ago. We used to dance at home. My grandfather used to come there and after supper, we'd get him to sing and the three of us would dance around the table. My grandson out there, he was standing there all by himself and all of a sudden he started bouncing and then he would quit again, and look around and see if anybody is dancing with him, and they would be, and he likes that.

The renowned choreographer Martha Graham once said that 'Dance is the hidden language of the soul, of the body.' It does not lie. Dance is another of those primitive impulses that free the spirit and let us engage in a dialogue with intangible aspects of creation. It is a unique type of communication that forms bonds with others that cannot be achieved with words. Dance even has the power to transform a person and to permanently raise one's level of consciousness. This type of dance, in which the whole body succumbs to irresistible driving rhythms for long periods of time in a shared and meaningful social context, is an ancient source of happiness. It can still be found in some non-Western settings.

In the West, some young people take lots of flak for their rave parties in which long hours of intense dance is part of the consciousness-altering experience. But when you cut through the drugs and youthful rebellion that goes along with it, ravers are only sampling an historical form of experience that once played a central role in the healthy exercise of human emotion. Happy societies make plenty of time for healthy raving.

Like dance, touch is one of the oldest forms of communication, and one of the richest veins of happiness. The first thing that hit me when I landed in Africa to take up my teaching post was how often, and how generously, people would touch each other. Upon being introduced to me, my teaching assistant shook my hand, and then continued to hold it for the next thirty minutes while giving me a tour of the campus. Everywhere, men could be seen holding hands and hanging off of each other. Women, young and old, always seemed to be locked on to one another.

After a couple of weeks, it dawned on me that I never heard babies crying. Dare I say that the babies were happy? The main reason, I believe, was the constant physical contact that they received all day long. At the many dance halls in the bush that I frequented with an anthropologist friend of mine, mothers even danced with the child strapped to their backs. Compared to that, people in most Western countries are on a severe starvation diet when it comes to touch, one more reason that we are always crying for something. Touch deprivation is one of the reasons for the many psychological and social ills that have befallen modern society.

Touch is the unspoken language of love and respect that has tremendous healing power, as well as the power to reduce stress and anxiety. It is essential for overall happiness, regardless of one's age. As a species, we were designed to touch. It is vital to our emotional and physical development. Medical researchers are turning increasingly to the use of touch therapies to aid in various types of treatment. Every study conducted on this subject shows that touch has positive emotional outcomes.

Happiness Key

Music expresses that which cannot be put into
words and that which cannot remain silent.

– VICTOR HUGO

As with dance and touch, music is frequently a high priority in
happy societies. One sees this very clearly in Latin American
and African countries, but many others as well. As Victor
Hugo wrote, music is about modes of expression that transcend
language, yet demand to be heard. Music is a cultural language
that evolves in all healthy societies. It transports a person to
depths of emotional experience that otherwise would not be
possible. Music melds together different parts of our being and
helps to organise human experience. Yehudi Menuhin, the
brilliant musician, writer and historian, gave us some of the
finest insights into the role of music in human history. In *The
Music of Man* he writes about music's higher-order functions:
'Music creates order out of chaos, for rhythm imposes
unanimity upon the divergent, melody imposes continuity
upon the disjointed, and harmony imposes compatibility upon
the incongruous.'

In many traditional societies, music had magical properties
that were seen as the means by which to contact the spirit
world, and to connect the past with the present. It has the
potential to make a large contribution to the well-being of
people within a society if it is able to contribute to social and
spiritual harmony, as it did in ages past. Music can add to
our sense of meaning. It can also enhance our appreciation
of beauty. For today's younger generation, music has become
largely a visual experience that is accessed by way of music

videos and other visual media. In terms of 'cultured' music, it is virtually impossible for a composer of orchestral music to be taken seriously if it contains any hint of tonality, harmony, or melody. One contemporary composer who recently received lots of world-wide media attention was someone whose 'music' involved screeching a violin bow along the wire of an outback fence in Australia.

Music has been gravitating for several decades away from the original purposes and potentialities of music, and becoming increasingly disjointed, aggressive, and noise-like. The abrasive and dissonant nature of today's music is often forgiven by calling it 'contemporary'. But it reflects the discords and despair that underlie the cultural crisis that is making people, like the music, cold and pointless. Menuhin mourns the trashing of historical forms of music in saying 'the tragedy today is that our civilisations are competing with each other most rapidly and effectively to destroy man's innate sense of the good, that good which is a composite of living purpose, fairness, and equilibrium'. The music of a society gives clues to the way in which people's emotions, as well as their happiness, are orchestrated and experienced. The woeful music consumed today is unable to perform any of its former roles in the creation of positive emotion. Much of it is depressing. Most of it is boring. Some of it is scary.

The Philippines comes to mind immediately when I think of a society that is still somewhat alive with music. One is almost never out of earshot of music there, whether one is walking through a village or down an alley of a big city. The Filipinos are also worth mentioning here for reasons other than their close connections to music. Happiness is a highly valued part of their national identity. In conversations, they are quick to proclaim that they are the happiest people in the world. In his article 'Our National Identity: A Most Happy People', Fred de la Rosa, editor-in-chief of the *Manila Times*, writes that their high level of happiness stems in part from their ability to be pleased with their lot in life.

There is even a popular catchphrase 'mababaw ang kaligayahan ng mga Pinoy' that translates into 'Filipinos are easy to please'. As de la Rosa says, 'we don't expect much. We think small'. Another phrase that is heard all the time is 'ok lang' which means 'it's ok, no big deal', which expresses how even very difficult situations are taken in easy stride. The Filipinos also have an exceptionally well-developed sense of humour that has evolved as a survival strategy. They are another example of a people whose amplified capacity for happiness is a response to adverse circumstances that would otherwise detract from happiness. Once again we see that emotional hardiness and the human capacity for happiness is actually strengthened by some amount of trial and tribulation.

The Philippines is a unique blend of cultural influences, with Malay roots that fused with Catholic traditions as well as the fiesta and siesta elements of Spanish conquerors. While people in certain other societies may be more visibly affected by happiness, it is hard to miss the 'obstinate cheerfulness', as it is sometimes called, of the Filipinos. There have been a number of happiness surveys that found Filipinos to have the highest percentage of 'very happy' people in Asia. They were also not far from the top in this regard in the World Values Survey.

Filipe de Leon, a professor of Filipinology at Manila University, is convinced that the claim of exceptionally high levels of happiness among the Filipino population is a real phenomenon. He feels that it is owing to a theme within Filipino culture known as 'kapwa', which is the Tagalog word that means 'shared being'. More than anything else, Filipino happiness is a social happiness. People there rarely do anything alone. They thrive in each other's company. The Philippines is one of the most open and socially inclusive societies in the world, and almost exactly opposite to the individualistic Western societies that make privacy a high priority as they pursue personal fulfilment. Yet they are also unlike most collectivist societies that emphasise 'face', status, and hierarchy.

Traditionally, Filipinos did not distinguish their own identity from that of the group. Of this, de Leon says 'the strongest social urge of the Filipino is to connect, to become one with people'. It is a mindset that inclines them to share everything, no matter how small or large. This involves some costs and sacrifices. But it is the source of feelings of collective strength, and serves to immunise people from loneliness, alienation, and the fears that accompany individualistic journeys through life. In summing up Filipino happiness, and happiness generally, de Leon states 'Togetherness is happiness. It might sound too obvious, almost banal, to point out had not so many people across the world forgotten it.'

In his article 'Why Filipinos Are Happy', veteran Filipino journalist Federico Pascual describes how sharing among the Filipinos extends to total strangers. Even the trend toward 'bayanihan' – which refers to the practice of individuals moving to another country to earn money to send back to the family – is motivated by the oneness that the person feels with the family. It is seen as a gesture of love and another means of expressing their togetherness. The actual word bayanihan means togetherness.

It is often said that happiness for the Filipinos is to be with the family. The family itself is a sort of paradigm for the entire culture. The term 'sacred familism' is sometimes used by sociologists to describe the profoundly deep-seated family values that create a foundation for personal and social well-being among Filipinos. In recent years, this has been shifting gradually toward a 'secular familism' that is more closely connected to material success. As this happens, it may come at a cost to the happiness in which Filipinos take considerable pride.

We are only in the beginning stages of learning how to locate cultures that are more favourable to happiness than others. Common sense tells us that some of the initial findings are rather dubious. For instance, no one actually believes that Switzerland has nearly double the number of 'very happy' people than across the border in France, or that Spain has almost twice as many 'very happy' people as neighbouring Portugal. But this is what the above-mentioned World Values Survey showed. The Americans came out significantly ahead of the Canadians. Great Britain, which no one ever accused of being a happy nation, had nearly three times as many 'very happy' people as Italy, which is often thought of as a country of buoyant, life-loving, and passionate people. Obviously a lot of refinement is needed when it comes to measuring happiness from one society to the next.

The data from the World Values Survey can be easily adjusted in a way that sends African and Latin American countries down the list and replaces the top spots with a completely different set of countries that do not have reputations as especially happy ones. Instead of using the data to compare nations on the basis of the percentage of 'very happy' people, some researchers created a formula that would penalise countries for having people who scored in the 'not very happy' and 'not at all happy' ranges. As it turns out, the societies with the highest percentage of 'very happy' people tend to have a greater proportion of people in the 'unhappy' ranges as well. Extremes of poverty undoubtedly play a role in this, as well as the fact that people in many non-Western societies feel less stigmatised in admitting that they might not be happy. When the handicapping formula was used, Iceland came out on top, followed closely by several northern European countries including Denmark, Sweden, The Netherlands, and Norway. Bunched in with the others at the top were also Switzerland, Ireland, Australia, and Great Britain. Venezuela dropped down to tenth place, and Nigeria fell to thirty-seventh.

While all Western consumer cultures share roughly the same underlying value systems, it is not entirely fair to lump them together and assume that they all offer the same prospects for happiness. One could do some hair-splitting, for example, and ask why Iceland is apparently slightly happier than the United States, or other Western nations. Firstly, it should be noted that the celebrations following reports of Iceland as the world's happiest country were rained upon when the media released statistics showing that Icelanders are some of the world's biggest consumers of anti-depressant medication. This confirmed some people's suspicions that they were just another depression- and suicide-prone northern European country that, if anything, should be on the list of the world's most emotionally dreary places. It is true that inhabitants of northern European countries carry the stereotype of being severe, emotionally inhibited unless intoxicated, and hyper-concerned with efficiency and punctuality. While as false and misleading as all stereotypes, it nonetheless made it difficult for people to think of these countries as the happiest ones of all.

To walk down the streets of towns and cities in Iceland, one is not bowled over by outward signs of happiness, as one would be in parts of Polynesia or Africa where happiness is intensely social. Some Icelanders describe themselves as a people who prefer to be judged by their work and level of craftsmanship rather than their social and personal traits. Others have said that their happiness is aided by the fact that they are few in number, homogenous, relatively young, and an island nation. They have the highest standard of living in the world according to some surveys. Icelanders have high educational standards and a zero illiteracy rate. Most speak several languages and are well informed and well travelled. In short, one could say that they have a lot about which to be happy.

Aida Sigmundsdottir is a social commentator who has written about Iceland's title as the world's 'happiest country' in relation to its history and national character, which is full of contradictions. She makes the point that Iceland has evolved variations of capitalism that have retained in people a strong commitment to social justice, as well as a sense of community and belongingness. Interestingly, she refers to their proneness toward excesses. Alcohol has long been one of these excesses, and their 'under the influence' antics are legendary. More recently, writes Sigmundsdottir, Icelanders have come to approach work and consumerism in increasingly fanatical ways. On the subject of their skyrocketing materialism, she observes that Icelanders have become compulsive in their spending habits and their desire to snap up new gadgets and fashions. Staying on top of the latest consumer trends has become the national pastime, and one that is pushing Icelanders to work longer and longer hours.

But there is a sprouting awareness in Icelandic society that people's growing devotion to work and consumption is threatening their well-being. Companies and businesses within Iceland have come to expect employees, especially men, to be on hand almost continuously. This has led to new types of family conflict and stress-related personal problems. Sigmundsdottir is hopeful that steps can be taken to reverse this trend before it further erodes the happiness of the people. But in many respects, what is happening to happiness in Iceland is happening to varying degrees in all Western countries that have come to define happiness by way of unsuccessful success. It has just taken a bit longer there to have an effect.

CHAPTER SIXTEEN

Mountains of Happiness

ALTHOUGH we talk about high levels of happiness in most of our modern Western societies, it is not until we learn about a place like the small Tibetan nation of Ladakh that we realise we have been scrounging on emotional crumbs. Anyone wanting to enter into a serious study of happiness should begin with Helena Norberg-Hodge's book *Ancient Futures*, which gives a detailed first-hand look at pre-1980 Ladakh. It is one of the most complete accounts of what I would call a happy society. Changes that have taken place since 1980 have already stripped away much of its magic, and there is no doubt that the Ladakhis are less happy than their pre-development and pre-tourism days. But this tragedy can also help us to better understand happiness, as well as its fragile nature.

Norberg-Hodge spent the better part of twenty years studying the Ladakhi people. She describes them as a deeply happy and contented people who lived in near-perfect harmony with their harsh environment. Prior to her contact with this inspirational society, she was of the opinion that happiness was largely determined by genetic and biological factors. But she writes that her time in Ladakh taught her that culture plays a far more fundamental role in determining the quality of emotional life.

Contributing to the exceptional well-being of these people was a social structure that resulted in profound respect for children and old people, a healthy sense of community, zero crime, no abuse of power, virtually no violence or aggression, no poverty, a high degree of sharing, and a strongly ingrained tolerance that eliminated most forms of social conflict. When asked why they never got upset or frustrated with their neighbours, the usual answer was 'We just live with each other, that's all.'

Whenever there was a threat of social friction, a third party, or 'spontaneous intermediary', would intervene and settle matters before they amounted to anything. Children as young as five years of age had already learned to step in to mediate squabbles between other children. Social harmony, politeness, empathy, kindness, compassion, sharing, and enlightenment were the values given greatest emphasis. The worst insult one could give to another person was to refer to them as 'one who angers easily'. A lack of pride was considered a virtue. In the words of Norberg-Hodge, they needed no additional forms of self-enhancement since 'their respect is so deep-seated as to be unquestioned'.

In the Buddhist tradition, the main enemy of happiness was seen as the individual ego. Children were often given names that meant victorious in the sense of having conquered the evil of ego. The Cham dance, an important annual Ladakhi event on the spiritual calendar, was a dramatic symbolic display of the killing of the ego.

Much of the work of these primarily rural people was shared, either at the organised community level or in smaller, less formal groups referred to as *chutso*. Grazing animals were shepherded in a communal way. Everyone owned their own sections of land, but private property was shared if it worked to the advantage of others, especially during harvest time. Draft animals and working tools were also shared. Competition had virtually no relevance to the society. The economy itself was founded on mutual cooperation, which was organised in both formal and informal ways.

While work could be strenuous during the four months of growing and harvesting, people's attitude toward work was lackadaisical and carried out at a leisurely pace that allowed people of all ages to keep up. They always sang as they worked, in particular the song that translates into 'make it easy, easy does it'. The work itself was mixed in with laughter and play. Ladakh was a culture that lacked a clear distinction between work and play.

The remaining eight months of the year demanded only minimal amounts of work. It was limited to daily chores of cooking, fetching water, and feeding the animals. Large amounts of time were left for family and community activities, as well as story-telling which was a traditional winter pastime, as well as a means by which to connect young and old alike with aspects of traditional culture. Singing together was a popular family activity, with many songs of a spiritual nature that reinforced Buddhist themes of wisdom, honesty, and respect for nature. This long stretch of the year was filled with all sorts of celebrations that followed one after the other. Music, drama, and dance featured abundantly in most of these events.

The impulse to share revealed itself at a very early age. A young child with a biscuit could be seen breaking it into little pieces and giving them to friends and siblings. Norberg-Hodge recalls a number of incidents in which two children sharing a plate of food both refused to eat the best piece of food on the plate in the hopes that the other one would eat it. The all-pervasive trait of sharing was a rich source of happiness and security for the people, as well as a means by which to express and receive recognition.

Children were spoiled in that they grew up with unlimited and unconditional affection, as well as constant physical contact. Mothers and children were never apart. In addition, other members of the family or local community were always on hand to help feed, cuddle, and play with the child. Young children participated in all adult activities, even late-night festivities. The idea of putting a child to bed at a fixed time was totally alien. Men as well as women were openly adoring of young children. Even teenage boys felt no embarrassment in fawning over children. The masculine identity of Ladakhi boys was not threatened by displays of tenderness.

On one occasion, Norberg-Hodge described to a Ladakhi mother how much time Western mothers spend away from their young children. The woman was overcome with sadness. She pleaded 'Please, *atche* Helena, when you have children, whatever you do, don't treat your baby like that. If you want a happy baby, do like we do.' By all accounts, the happy Ladakhi babies turned into happy adults. Rather than tending toward narcissism, these spoiled Ladakhi children quickly developed their own sense of social responsibility that saw them join in as caretakers by the age of five or six.

Women grew up to be strong, self-assured, dignified, and fun-loving. They were confident and relaxed in their interactions with men. People of both sexes developed into generalists who were capable of functioning in a wide variety of roles. Sex role differences were minimal, as were the tensions that arose from these. An unmistakable sense of equality permeated through the entire society. There were no 'Joneses', and no one experienced any preoccupations with their rank or status. Even the authorities were local people or groups who were regarded as friends rather than any sort of policing agents.

Initially, Norberg-Hodge found their vitality and consistent high spirits to be a bit too good to be true: 'At first I couldn't believe that the Ladakhis could be as happy as they appeared. It took me a long time to accept that the smiles I saw were real.' As time went on, she came to appreciate the special cultural blueprints that maximised their potential for happiness. She wrote of them:

> I have never met people who seem so healthy emotionally, so secure, as the Ladakhis. You cannot spend any time at all in Ladakh without being won over by the contagious laughter. The Ladakhis possess an irrepressible *joie de vivre* (joy of living). Their sense of joy seems so firmly anchored within them that circumstances cannot shake it loose.

The passage below tells part of the story of the exquisite harmony that was played out at several levels of their lives, which speaks of a happiness that was balanced across the full range of human and environmental needs:

> The Ladakhis belong to their place on earth. They are bonded to that place through intimate daily contact, through a knowledge about their immediate environment with its changing seasons, needs, and limitations. They are aware of the

living context in which they find themselves. The movement of the stars, the sun, and moon are familiar rhythms that influence their daily activities.

The bodies of the Ladakhis were also a source of well-being, vigour, and pleasure. Nearly everyone was fit, with almost no one underweight or overweight. Obesity was unheard of. Men as well as women were strong and worked until the time of their deaths. They did have a fairly high infant mortality rate, especially in very harsh winters, but general health was remarkably good once past the initial critical years. Their physical health was assisted by relaxed lifestyles low in stress, and high in peace of mind. By today's standards, their diets were far too high in cholesterol and salt, but they seemed to suffer none of the Western-style consequences such as heart disease.

Their mental health was unsurpassed, with no evidence of Western-style neuroses, depression, or anxiety disorders. Postnatal depression was non-existent. They enjoyed an inner contentment that could not be ruined by outside events. The intimate bonds that they had forged with one another had the effect of keeping them happy, calm, and serene under virtually any circumstances. Even nasty predicaments, such as the loss of most of one's crops, were shrugged off easily, and often turned into sources of jest. Norberg-Hodge came to the conclusion that large extended families within small-scale communities are the best building blocks for well-balanced, free, independent, and happy people: 'A healthy society is one that encourages close social ties and mutual interdependence, granting each individual a net of unconditional emotional support. Paradoxically, I have found the Ladakhis less emotionally dependent than we are in industrial society.'

The insulation that Ladakhi culture offered from emotional pain was also in evidence with physical pain. One day, while wading barefooted across a snow-fed mountain stream with a Ladakhi woman, Norberg-Hodge was amazed that the woman was completely unfazed by the icy temperature of the water. When Norberg-Hodge exclaimed something to the effect 'Wow, don't you find that cold?!', the woman had no idea of what she meant by that question. The water was simply a part of her reality, and as such required no critical evaluation. She had also not been sensitised to pain by its continual avoidance.

The respect that was shaped into the Ladakhis showed through in their compassionate treatment of all life forms. With one another, they held back from imposing absolute judgements, always opting to say that any opinion was theirs and theirs alone. In asking a Ladakhi if the sky is big, you are likely to get an answer along the lines of 'It seems so to me.' This lack of presumptuousness showed through in their veneration of nonhuman animals.

It was taught to them from a young age that no one had the right to take even the life of an insect unless it was essential to do so. For this reason, they chose only the largest animals to kill for eating since the taking of a single life was more compassionate than the taking of many lives, as would be the case with a plate of small fish. On certain special occasions, such as weddings, no one would work the fields in case they would accidentally kill an insect or other innocent creatures, which was thought to be a bad omen. When an animal had to be killed, a prayer was said asking for forgiveness and wishing that the animal would quickly reach Buddhahood.

If the Ladakhis were frugal when it came to the wasting of

lives, they were at least as frugal when it came to other areas of their lives. Frugality and conservation-mindedness were sources of joy and spiritual richness for the Ladakhis. We in the consumption-driven West have come to attach negative connotations to frugality, rather than viewing it according to its original meaning of 'fruitfulness' and 'sparing'. The idea of frugality has also lost all meaning in terms of how we approach happiness. But Elise Boulding, a sociologist and author of *Cultures of Peace*, points out that the ethos of consumerism has actually done a tragic disservice to our prospects for happiness by discounting the value of this form of consciousness: 'Frugality is one of the most beautiful and joyful words in the English language, and yet one that we are culturally cut off from understanding and enjoying. The consumption society has made us feel that happiness lies in having things, and has failed to teach us the happiness of not having things.'

In Ladakhi society, waste of any sort was seen as a form of ugliness and cruelty. It was an insult to life, as well as a display of stupidity. Only a buffoon would squander a resource or toss out something that was of use to another person, animal, or plant. In many ways, life was a prayer for the Ladakhis, with frugality being an important voice in this prayer, as well as a part of their survival. The Ladakhis would even strain their dishwater to remove any small morsels of food that could be given to the animals. An act like this went beyond the requirements of their survival. To do that was an extension of their belief system in which waste avoidance was regarded as a show of respect for life itself. It was a gesture of kindness of the type preached in the Buddhist religion that interspersed with their daily lives.

While we may snicker at the idea of saving tiny food scraps, the Ladakhis experienced it with a sense of beauty. They found descriptions of the waste and disregard for resources in Western societies to be completely implausible. They assumed it to be a joke. In a sense, the Ladakhis had managed what some visionaries are now calling the spiritually based 'sustainable happiness' that must eventually replace the haphazard feel-good-at-any-cost model of happiness that presides in consumer culture.

The depth of spirituality of the Ladakhis, like the depth of their social connectedness, had the effect of taking the sting out of life's setbacks. Even death was taken in their stride more readily than in the West, where death has become an enemy that wants to steal our most prized possession – ourselves. Curiously, Ladakhi religion itself was lived out with a casualness that seemed to mock its high status. Even a visit by the Dalai Lama did not get people over-excited, as would a visit by the Pope to a Western country. This was because religion was not separate from the rest of their lives, which means that they felt no need to act it out with any special theatrics. Religion was not compartmentalised into a one hour per week melodrama and social outing. Instead, it percolated in subtle ways throughout all actions of mind and body. The regular practice of meditation for ordinary people was far more subtle and informal than the stereotyped practice of it that we know of in the West. Everything was kept simple.

Happiness Key
Simplicity is the ultimate sophistication.

– LEONARDO DA VINCI

The entire constellation of Ladakhi cultural values seemed to combine in their ability to feel blessed with the way things were. Whereas we are drawn like magnets toward destabilising complication, simplicity was part of their collective wisdom. In the modern dash for more and better, we often underestimate the degree of intelligence that is required to remain simple. Leonardo da Vinci makes this point when he describes simplicity as a high form of sophistication. Similarly, in *Small is Beautiful*, E. F. Schumacher writes 'Any fool can make things bigger, more complex, and more violent. It takes a touch of genius – and a lot of courage – to move in the opposite direction.'

Catastrophe struck in the early 1980s when Ladakh was finally gripped by the tentacles of consumer capitalism. Since then their lives have become increasingly fast, stressful, complicated, competitive, and self-centred. Crime reared its head with a vengeance. Norberg-Hodge writes correctly that modern Western culture looks better from the outside than it feels from the inside. But Ladakhis had to learn this for themselves. Once they were exposed to digital watches and soup-in-a-cup, they began to feel poor by contrast. A belching slug of stomach-burning Coca-Cola was suddenly more satisfying than a drink of their traditional lingonberry juice. Tight-fitting, over-priced jeans began feeling better than comfortable cotton saris and warm fleece robes. For the first time, money and false needs began to frame their outlook on the world.

Overseers of Ladakh's first stages of development in the early 1980s were concerned that Ladakhi culture lacked the psychological infrastructure that could generate enough greed in order to get a consumer economy growing. For instance, in 1981, Ladakh's Development Commissioner made the statement 'If Ladakh is ever going to be developed we have to figure out how to make these people more greedy. You just can't motivate them otherwise.' But greed promoters triumphed and a greed economy took root. The following words from one Ladakhi woman attests to the arrival of this murderous god: 'It's terrible, everyone is getting so greedy. Money was never important before, but now it's all people can think about.' Today, the new issues are unemployment, the widening gap between rich and poor, the breakdown of family life, pollution, sprawl, and out-of-control development. This comes with the usual benefits afforded by progress, technology, and education.

The Ladakhis are an example of a society that requires us to question our basic assumptions about progress and development as they impact upon human well-being. In his book *What Does Development Mean?*, economist Ted Trainer refers to the Ladakhis as an example of a 'superior culture' that was populated by 'notoriously happy people' who had no need whatsoever for televisions, computers, cars, supermarkets, disposable products, higher incomes, or enlarged gross domestic product. Without all these trappings, he adds, they thrived in an exquisitely developed culture that offered a rich social and spiritual life, efficient and sustainable food production, and a relaxed lifestyle that left copious amounts of free time for the smaller joys of daily life. While some say it is too late, there are projects under way in Ladakh to help stem the cultural and environmental destruction that has wiped the smile off the faces of so many of these beautiful people.

The clash that took place in Ladakh between happiness and modernisation is the stuff about which many books could be written. Without going further into it here, there is a small section toward the end of Norberg-Hodge's book that sums up the tragedy of Ladakh quite poignantly. During her first years in Ladakh, young children that she had never met before would come up to her and press apricots into her hands. It was simply a gesture of sharing and kindness. Today, she writes, children of the same age, wearing tattered Western-style clothes, rush up with empty outstretched hands, hoping for a handout. The glitter is gone from their eyes.

From several standpoints, pre-1980 Ladakh was a type of Eden that offered one of the best recipes for emotional and mental well-being. In undergoing the modern version of The Fall, it entered into the type of captivity that yields the lacklustre brand of happiness of which most of us can stake some claim. For some reason, Ladakh was especially vulnerable to the forces of modernisation, and it disintegrated quickly. But there are a few remaining 'happy societies' that have been partially able to slow the loss of happiness that has resulted from contact with the smiling assassin.

CHAPTER SEVENTEEN
Oceans of Happiness

SOME of the happiest people in the world today live in the villages of the 'Happiness Triangle', made up of Samoa, Fiji, and Tonga. Samoa in particular has been acclaimed for hundreds of years as a society of happiness and joy. I will focus here on Samoa, but much of what I say also applies to Fiji and Tonga, which share many common features with Samoa and are both renowned for their happiness.

My first contact with people from the Happiness Triangle was on a trip to Fiji. Upon my arrival, I rented a car and began driving through a torrential rainstorm en route to a remote part of the main island. Unable to see, I pulled to the side of the road, only to be greeted by a group of women and children who were laughing and joking next to a stack of papaws that they were selling. I rolled down the window a crack and rain pelted in, but I thought I would do them a favour by buying some fruit, which I did. As we did our exchange, I struggled to understand why they were so outrageously happy. When I drove away, I said 'Horrible day, isn't it?', to which one of the women replied 'Sega na Lega.'

Further up the road, the rain got even worse and I pulled over next to a bridge that crossed a small but fast-flowing flooded river. By that point I was really worried about the conditions ahead and if I would make it to Raki Raki by nightfall. Then to my horror, I caught a brief glimpse of a small boy floating at high speed down the river. I jumped out of the car, only to hear the sounds of laughter as a bunch of other rapturous children flashed down the river, each clinging to an irregular-shaped chunk of styrofoam. A man soon appeared at my side and my first comment was 'Isn't that dangerous?', to which he chuckled and replied 'Sega na Lega', which I later learned was an all-pervasive cultural motto meaning 'No problem'. Since that initial encounter, my experiences with the villagers of Fiji have convinced me beyond any doubt that they enjoy a level and quality of happiness that has been lost in the Western world. This may even be truer of the Samoans who are renowned, historically, for their prodigious happiness.

The journals of the first missionaries to Samoa in the 1830s allude to the flagrant happiness of the healthy 'heathens' who lived in picturesque dwellings surrounded by breadfruit and coconut groves. John Stair, a missionary who lived in Samoa from 1838 to 1845, was especially struck by the people's 'great want of co-operation' and their preference for simplicity which caused the locals to be 'sorely puzzled with European complications'. The one aspect of Samoan life that did strike Stair as over-complicated was the elaborate rules of social etiquette that were a constant part of daily life. While he assumed that this must have been 'excessively irksome and oppressive' for the locals, he was in fact observing a social system that to this day works very well at distributing happiness evenly across the entire society.

Sometimes it is jokingly said that, in Samoa, there is never a problem of finding the Chief, or 'Alii'. The problem is more of finding someone who is not a Chief of some sort. Copious amounts of respect are bestowed upon one another in the course of everyday conversation, with people referring to each other as 'Alii', which can also mean 'Sir', 'Lord', or 'Gentleman'. Even children can be heard addressing each other in this way. The language and customs do not lend themselves to the concept of a commoner, or someone who is excluded from the fold. This inalienable right of inclusion certainly plays into the feelings of shared happiness about which the Samoans pride themselves.

Author Robert Louis Stevenson fell in love with the happiness and warm spirit of the Samoans and ended up living among them until the time of his death in 1894. Known to the people as Tusitala, or 'story-teller', Stevenson commented many times on their extraordinary ability to savour all aspects of life. He nicknamed the Samoans 'the happy people'. Samoa is even referred to frequently as Motu o fiafiaga, or 'Island of Happiness'. It is also known to many of us as 'The Land of No Worries'. One never goes long without hearing 'Aua le popole ae fiafia', or 'Don't worry, be happy', which was their motto long before these words were popularised in the West.

Stevenson's views on happiness seem to have been shaped by his contact with the Samoans. He once said 'There is no duty we so underrate as the duty of being happy. By being happy we sow benefits upon the whole world.' In this way, the happiness that is spread generously within Samoan society is understood as a type of social obligation that is good for the whole 'family'.

The word 'aiga, which means 'family', is the first thing that comes to mind when Samoans are asked to explain their high degree of collective happiness. They have a saying along the lines of 'There is no other place in the world except the family.' The 'aiga is of major psychological importance to Samoans. It is a far-reaching force that is experienced as a source of meaning, continuity, belonging, and security. The strong cultural emphasis on happiness is really about maintaining a happy 'aiga, or family.

The Samoan family is a much deeper and wider institution than the flimsy one that hangs on by a thread in consumer culture. It is a multi-layered one that consists of the immediate extended family, the nu'u (i.e. village), as well as every Samoan living anywhere in Samoa or abroad. From a young age, children are able to describe the family 'gafa', or genealogy, from both sides of the family. They quickly become familiar with stories and legends that relate to the family, the nu'u, and the Samoan nation. These 'fagogo', or traditional stories, are usually accompanied by song and told at night. They are seen as an important means by which children are instilled with moral sensibilities.

Very few elements of competition or greed have found their way into this expanded family structure. Sharing extends to people who are not members of the immediate family. A good catch of fish, for example, will often be distributed to other members of the community, with first portions going to anyone in special need.

Being a stranger does not exclude a person from the family, even when they live a long distance away. In New Zealand, which has a large Samoan population, it is common practice for people to travel to another part of the country to attend the funeral of another Samoan who has died, even though they know nothing about the deceased person except that he or she was part of the global Samoan 'aiga.

A Samoan walking through a village where he or she is not known is likely to hear someone call out the words 'sau e ai', or 's'us'u mai e taumafa'. These are, respectively, the informal and formal ways of saying 'Come and eat.' This happens with strangers and friends alike. I have spoken to Samoans who say that this can happen with such frequency that a person has to eat only small amounts of food at each house in order not to become so full as to insult someone by not being able to share their food.

Happiness is considered to be a great event in Samoa. In the tradition of naming children after such events, you will find that quite a few people in Samoa are named Fiafia, which means happy. The Samoans describe happiness in a way that does not sound like the personal happiness of isolated individuals, as we think of it in the West. They usually refer to it as a sort of collective celebration.

Among the Samoans I interviewed about the edge that they have in terms of happiness was Methodist minister Reverend Sa'ai'u Ale Palelei, who had a thorough appreciation of the unique foundations of Samoan happiness. He described the many occasions on which Samoans come together in groups in order to make each other happy. Herein probably lies the key to Samoan happiness, since one's own happiness seems inextricably linked to others being happy, or being able to make someone else happy.

The culture itself has evolved formal group practices, such as the 'Faa Tau Pati' or 'Slap Dance', that originated as tools for lifting up each other's spirits. Reverend Pelelei pointed out that Samoans are more than willing to have their houses turned inside out and their gardens levelled, as long as a group of visitors are happy and full of joy. But these group forays do not have the same flavour as a party in modern Western culture, which usually amounts to inebriated acquaintances lapsing into pretence and exhibitionism. Instead, they have to some extent the tone of a spiritual revival that has a lot to do with rejoicing and giving thanks.

Here too lies another key to understanding Samoan happiness. It cannot be separated from religion, in the same way that it cannot be separated from family and community. When Samoans are asked about the percentage of people who are religious and attend church on a regular basis, the answer is always the same: 'Everybody'. That sounds a bit far-fetched but it is true. Religion is said by Samoans to be the glue that unites all of the institutions and practices that enable their particular socio-spiritual version of happiness. Most of them agree that, without that strength of religious conviction, they would not be known as Motu o fiafiaga.

In 1963, the famous anthropologist Margaret Mead was asked the question 'Is there any one society that you have observed in which the people seem considerably happier than those in other societies?' Her reply was 'A happy society would be one like Samoa.' Even though her book *Coming of Age in Samoa* was criticised for her less than perfect research methods that led her to conclude that Samoans did not suffer any of the adolescent stresses and sexual hang-ups of the West, she was certainly accurate in her perception of Samoa as a society that generates more than its share of positive emotion. It is still possible to see clearly what Mead was describing as 'the pleasant mild round of their way of life' and a society that 'emphasized a graceful, easy, diffused emotional life, and a relaxed dependence upon reliable social forms'. It was these sorts of observations that led her to describe Samoan culture as one that promoted happiness, contentment, and 'the greatest degree of mental health in its members'.

Some people have wondered why Samoa has been able to remain relatively happy in the face of modernisation, unlike Ladakh and many other casualties of progress, development, and technology. Interestingly, in the 1920s, Margaret Mead had already noticed that Samoan culture seemed to possess a wisdom that allowed it to filter out the toxic elements of other cultures and to retain those which could benefit their own. The last lines of Mead's book read: 'The Samoans have only taken such parts of our culture as made their life more comfortable, their culture more flexible, the concept of the mercy of God without the doctrine of original sin.'

In the early 1980s, Samoan culture did come under some threat as the mass media brought about a shift in consciousness to all things 'palangi', or Caucasian. While 'palangi' continues to be an ongoing issue that needs to be dealt with by Samoans, their culture seems to have initiated what is sometimes called the 'reactionary thing' that causes people to critically compare outside cultural offerings in the context of their merits, or lack thereof, to Samoan society. We in the West generally think of ourselves as 'developed' but we too continue to be challenged by the pressures of development, which has ongoing implications for happiness. Our attitude has been passive and uncritical for the most part. But there could be a valuable lesson in the way in which a nation like Samoa can sift out the good from the bad, and reject some of which is unhealthy to their prospects for fiafiaga.

CHAPTER EIGHTEEN

The Future of Happiness

IN years to come it will be necessary to learn, and to teach, the importance of distinguishing between different types of happiness, while judging it on the basis of quality. Consumer culture does not prepare people to pursue a constructive happiness that can nourish them and make them relevant to the world. To be full of the wrong type of happiness is worse than having no happiness at all since it must be unlearned before the person can move on and begin to develop a worthwhile happiness. In the consumer age, we have been living like thieves, and stealing our happiness in a way that is not sustainable for individuals or the physical world upon which we depend for our survival.

While most do not realise it, we have come to the end of the road in terms of consumer happiness, which is a surface-level happiness that has alienated people from their basic natures. We find ourselves in a sea of happiness that would drain instantly if we were to pull the plug on televisions and shopping malls, or to pluck out the teat of work that suckles so many people emotionally. We are at a critical point in human history that is going to require tomorrow's people to find happiness in much healthier ways than today.

Later in his life, the famous humanistic psychologist Carl Rogers wrote about the importance of becoming a 'person of tomorrow' in order to arrive at a happiness that is superior to the type found in consumer society. Interestingly, he said that tomorrow's happiness would probably not be experienced at all like the happiness of today. The person of tomorrow may not even regard herself or himself as especially happy since their approach to life would be a growth-oriented one that regarded the good life as an ongoing process, rather than an incessant state of satisfaction or titillation.

The happiness of the person of tomorrow was seen by Rogers as the result of continually moving in the direction of caring, authenticity, wholeness, intimacy, and openness. It would also come by way of cultivating reverence for nature, learning the unimportance of material things, developing scepticism about technology and science as a harbinger of happiness, and expanding one's spiritual sensitivities. But this happiness was seen as possible only if individuals could shift authority to within themselves, while training themselves to become anti-institutional. This speaks of the fact that genuine happiness in today's world is a form of protest. Far more than a simple intellectual daily choice, it is a revolutionary response that calls upon the person to entertain doubt and to question the norms of their host culture.

Under healthy cultural conditions, it would not be necessary to engage in so-called 'deliberate living', in which one must consciously fend off threats to one's emotional welfare. But there is a growing minority of people who are now speaking of the need to society-proof themselves and their children in order to find a fulfilling happiness. Happiness achieved in this way takes a fair amount of determination, which is always the case when one is trying to be sane in an insane society. Nonetheless, society-proofing may be the only short-term option for people who want a high-quality happiness.

Happiness Key

Happiness is like those palaces in fairy tales whose gates are guarded by dragons: we must fight in order to conquer it.

— ALEXANDRE DUMAS

The words of nineteenth-century French playwright and novelist Alexandre Dumas have never been more relevant than today. It is not possible to slay the dragon of consumer culture by adjusting to its norms. Happiness in the current age requires a certain degree of ab-normality, even if people must feel themselves to be different.

Maladjustment seems to be an unlikely prescription for happiness. But there is wisdom in being at odds with norms that intercept us from an authentic happiness. A society that allows material things to take precedence over people is fatally flawed and not worthy of blind obedience. In *Escape From Freedom*, Erich Fromm wrote about the disobedience that was demanded of a person in a society that had become insane from the standpoint of our basic humanity: 'We can't make people sane by making them adjust to this society. We need a society that is adjusted to the needs of people.' Until society reinvents itself as a human enterprise, rather than an economic one, happiness and mental health will depend upon the ability to defend oneself against norm-ality.

The ability to generate new wealth is a great strength of radical consumerism, but it is quickly becoming our greatest weakness. The growth of economies is not being matched by a growth of wisdom about the way in which to utilise wealth. Without such wisdom, the amplification of wealth can easily magnify the already existing problems that plague the consumer age. Many people are drowning of thirst in a sea of fresh water. Ironically, it is their wealth that often serves to weight them down. What they really need is a new way to be rich.

In recent years, the small Tibetan nation of Bhutan has been making symbolic gestures to the rest of the world regarding the corrosive effects of rampant consumerism on the quality of social and spiritual life, as well as the health of the Earth's ecosystem. In defiance of the prevailing habit of gauging human happiness by economic measures, they made 'gross happiness product' the official measure of the health and well-being of their society. This has inspired a number of thinkers to reapproach happiness as a cultural product that can be influenced by broad social and political changes.

Ed Diener and Martin Seligman, both eminent theorists in the area of happiness, have argued that modern capitalistic societies should reassess their current economic methods of defining the so-called good life. In their *Psychological Science in the Public Interest* article 'Beyond Money: Toward an Economy of Well-Being', they urge governments and policy-makers to build in new measures of personal well-being in order to begin competing with the Dow Jones average, interest rate reports, consumer confidence statistics, and the role of money as the surrogate for core human needs. What we need, say Diener and Seligman, are new ways of measuring how well we are doing on such things as mental health, interpersonal relationships, trust between people, participation in the community, motivation for living, the prevention of boredom, the achievement of meaning and purpose, and an overall sense that life is a worthwhile experience.

Visions such as these are of utmost importance at a time when economic forces are on the verge of overshadowing all other reasons for existence. But governments are the biggest players in the happiness conspiracy. They are hugely invested in greed economics and consumption-based 'happiness'. This means that political changes aimed at encouraging a people-friendly and planet-friendly happiness are almost certain to be met with fierce resistance. This puts the onus back on the individual to seek happiness by way of rebellion.

Some people are beginning to form groups whose goal it is to actively challenge the norms of consumer culture. Among them are those who have embarked on a course of 'culture jamming', which targets the media and its relentless stream of messages telling us to seek happiness through the satisfaction of false needs. For instance, in his book *Culture Jam*, Kalle Lasn writes that happiness in America is almost impossible since 'America is no longer a country, but a multi-trillion dollar brand.' Because genuine happiness must have an ethical foundation, he adds, it is even more difficult because 'consumer capitalism is by its nature unethical', a point that is being echoed by a number of concerned social thinkers.

In saying that current formulas for living and for happiness are not sustainable, one has to assume that culture change will be necessary in order to avoid total catastrophe. Culture change activists play a small but positive role in hastening the inevitable corrections that must be made to our self-destructive cultural design. Western governments have been far too slow to promote the legislation that would help to halt the steady rise of social, environmental, and mental health problems. As just one small example, they have been completely impotent in trying to stem the flow of wasteful and polluting four-wheel drive SUVs onto our roads, the effect of which is billions of barrels of squandered oil. Environmental laws are being relaxed continually to allow oil companies to exploit the last remaining areas of pristine wilderness.

A large portion of today's consumer happiness is actually dependent upon oil. Closing the oil tap by even 25 per cent would be a devastating blow to people's sense of well-being and 'life satisfaction'. Yet, ironically, there are those who see the end of oily happiness as a favourable development that could bring about a type of happiness that corresponds more closely to our humanity. They argue that, since the political and economic mechanisms are not in place to cope with the imminent world-wide oil crisis, the mother of all economic depressions will root people out of the four-wheelers and traffic jams and onto bicycles and walkways. Conversation and story-telling will reappear as the work-addicted masses are forced back into the normal rhythms of human interaction.

From the ashes of this colossal upheaval would be born simpler and less work-driven lifestyles that are more conducive to happiness by way of its 'poverty'. A sluggish oil-free world might even be the collective excuse needed for the rise of an idleness ethic that would turn the tide on the unforgiving work ethic. This could constitute the partial realisation of the ideal society described by Bertrand Russell in *In Praise of Idleness* where he writes that 'the road to happiness and prosperity lies in an organized diminution of work'. The pent-up readiness that the modern person has for creative idleness can be seen in the runaway popularity of Tom Hodgkinson's recent book *How to Be Idle*. In there, he makes the case for a universal standard of living in which everyone is capable of being happy doing nothing. Such a foundation gives rise to a life rich in imagination, love, and play.

Jan Lundberg has written for years about the connection between oil and consumer-style happiness. He is a former oil industry analyst who founded the Sustainable Energy Institute, and currently heads an international group promoting culture change (www.culturechange.org). Lundberg came to realise that much of what we call happiness today is about to be shattered by the relatively sudden end that is coming to the era of fossil fuel. We are currently in the pre-collapse denial stage in which people are slightly anxious but still clinging to material hopes and technological illusions as a source of emotional nutrition. Because we are unprepared for the transition to an oil-free world, he foresees a considerable period of time in which people will be in a state of extreme strife and cultural disorientation.

Lundberg sees today's happiness as largely obsolete since so much of it unfolds against the backdrop of consumer spending and oppressive petroleum domination. In his essay 'The Awakening of the Downtrodden', he writes that we have become cornered animals whose only way out is to adopt a 'rebellious vision' that can reacquaint us with freedom and a more human mode of existence, even if that means a return to some of the ways of our ancient hunter-gatherer forbears.

The alternative 'ecotopia' that some futurists foresee replacing consumer happiness in an oil-less world would take us closer to the land and to the joys that arise when nature becomes the prime source of meaning. However, this human revolution would be impossible with the planet as vastly overpopulated as it is today. Overpopulation is the worst threat to overall human welfare and the prospects for future happiness. The end of the fossil-fuel period of history would set in motion a process of social evolution that would drastically reduce the numbers of people that inhabit the Earth.

The human population continues to grow at a killing pace. It is predicted to increase by nearly one billion people over the next decade. But as a prelude to what is ahead, one can already see depopulation trends emerging in some regions, most notably the European countries. While this is a positive development, we are so bogged down in economic definitions of human well-being that governments are lurching into plans that will reverse the trend. For instance, the German government announced recently that one of its main goals is to motivate people to have more children in order to safeguard the economy. But that is utterly futile since streamlined families are going to be a permanent feature of the future. By necessity, happiness itself will be simpler and more streamlined.

In the conclusion of *Darwinian Happiness*, Bjørn Grinde also sets out a utopian vision of future happiness that relies in large part on the depopulation of our species. The two genetic predispositions that he sees standing in the way of an eventual 'Paradise Society' that is ideally suited for human happiness are reproduction and selfishness. But Grinde has grave concerns that modern society is on track to turn the entire planet into a 'biological refuse dump' that will more closely resemble hell than paradise. In saying that 'today's societies resemble a zoo', he argues that the achievement of a truly human happiness cannot be found by following the lead of the current cultural zookeepers who are responsible for the ongoing societal breakdown. Among other things, he emphasises the need to rely more heavily on our free will in trying to find our way back to ourselves, and to a 'Darwinian' happiness that sustains life.

The futurists who predict that human happiness has no choice except to become greener and more sustainable sometimes point to traditional Mennonite culture as a prototype for tomorrow's happiness. Along with the Amish, who are a branch of the Mennonites, their society is predicated on a rejection of progress and modernisation. These groups have been receiving lots of attention in recent years from mental health professionals and happiness researchers. Old Order Mennonites have been found consistently to have exceptionally low rates of depression, suicide, substance abuse, marital conflict, and divorce. In 2002, researchers at the Canadian Institute for Health Information studied the physical health of traditional Mennonite children and found that both boys and girls were significantly fitter, leaner, and stronger than children raised in mainstream Canadian culture. It was calculated that the difference in caloric expenditure between the traditional Mennonite lifestyle and that of the modern Canadian was the equivalent of nineteen kilograms of body fat per person, per decade.

Unlike greed economics that views conservation as a threat, their economy thrives on it. Waste of any sort is actively discouraged. The amount of pollution per capita is only a small fraction of that produced by the modern consumer. Avarice and competitive conflict are almost non-existent.

Mennonite families are tightly knit extended ones that provide security for everyone regardless of age. The closely united community looks after all of its members in times of crisis, thus rendering insurance policies a meaningless concept. Poverty, crime, and violence are nowhere to be found. In the process of making the land into the focal point of their energies, they avoid the emotional toxicity of dehumanising corporations, large factories, technology chasing, and career ladder climbing. Children forego the fattening and brain-numbing fates of fast foods and passive electronic games. Education is done locally on a small scale, thus sparing children the dumbed-down type of learning that is designed to create clones suited for competitive rat racing. The entire workings of traditional Mennonite societies are enveloped in spirituality that gives meaning to their low-impact, sustainable, and morally grounded lifestyles.

But while they are undoubtedly superior in terms of mental health, physical well-being, and stewardship of the planet, are they happy? According to researchers, yes they are. The Mennonites consistently report high levels of happiness. They also made the news when their levels of life satisfaction were found to be as high as that reported by high-flyers on the 'Forbes 400' list of richest people. Of course, the humble nature of their happiness and satisfaction could not be much more different than that experienced by our celebrated corporate heroes, whose emotional worlds are governed largely by false profits. Personal profitability is lacking almost entirely from the Old Order Mennonite conception of happiness.

My own encounters with traditional Mennonites in Ontario, Canada and Indiana, USA have taught me that they enjoy a quiet but substantial type of happiness that eludes modernised consumption-driven individuals. Along with my wife, whose father was Mennonite, I would sometimes sit and talk to members of the local Mennonite community about their way of life and their outlook on the world. Before I came to understand them better, I assumed, like most people, that they were naïve about the world. That turned out to be completely false. But their lives are ideally suited to preserving a state of innocence and curiosity that keeps open a door to joy and wonder. In that respect, they are highly advanced.

In coming to appreciate Mennonite happiness, I discovered some of the other traits that have been cited as reasons for their exceptionally high degree of emotional well-being. Among these are generosity and a deep commitment to the service of others. As part of their reverence for the land, they live out a type of frugality that, like the Ladakhis, is a source of practical and spiritual meaning. It is uncertain how long the Mennonites and Amish can fend off the outside world of consumerism, which is trying to turn them into a tourist attraction. Greed-driven property development and investment has also caused land prices to skyrocket, which is forcing some of them into various types of cottage industries and small businesses.

The term 'sustainability' can be roughly defined as an environment that is adequate for the health, well-being, and happiness of all human beings, including future generations. To reach this, it seems unavoidable that some sacrifices must be made. But optimists are drawing on the 'biophilia hypothesis' in suggesting that it may not be overly difficult to make the transition from a destructive consumer happiness to one that entails patterns of consciousness that are sane from a long-term ecological standpoint.

Biophilia literally means 'love of life'. The biophilia hypothesis recognises that, once humans become detached from their natural environment, it is possible for them to persist generation after generation in artificial lifestyles that are ultimately self-defeating at the individual and species level. When this occurs, as I believe it has today, people do not feel fully alive as human beings and have no way of getting in touch with their survival emotions, which hold the key to happiness. But those who foresee a future of happy biophiles point out studies showing the dramatic transformations that can occur when people suffering various symptoms of the 'modern person syndrome' (e.g. stress, anxiety, chronic fatigue, anger disorders, depression, etc.) are exposed for prolonged periods of time to wilderness conditions and other settings that restore atrophied human emotions.

Catherine O'Brien of Canada's Centre for Sustainable Transportation is the main developer of the concept of 'sustainable happiness'. The essential nature of this concept is revealed in a recent comment she made about the future of happiness: 'When our notion of happiness evolves to a more mature level we will understand happiness as an opportunity to create a gentler and more compassionate world where our happiness does not depend on exploiting people, the environment and future generations. This requires that we overcome our misguided thinking that happiness can be achieved through consumption and embrace the pursuit of sustainable happiness.'

Fear is the main obstacle preventing our happiness from growing up and becoming aligned to our natures, and to our requirements for survival. Most of us are victims of a culture of fear that has convinced us that we would starve emotionally if we did not consume our way through life.

Happiness Key

Happiness is a form of courage.

– HOLBROOK JACKSON

It does in fact take courage to be genuinely happy in today's world, as British historian Holbrook Jackson wrote. Fear is how we are shaped and controlled as consumers. Overcoming this is vital to the attainment of something more than a consumable happiness. But it is not surprising that most people are afraid to live the type of life that would bring about a genuine happiness. It is seen as too dangerous and too different. The majority of them prefer to live in confidence that they are successful servants than to embark upon a truer course of happiness.

There are a number of studies that have looked at why it is that people actually adopt materialistic attitudes and select lifestyles that revolve around overwork and excessive consumption. The findings tend to confirm that fear is one of the biggest reasons. Specifically, people report that they would feel ostracised, anxious, and embarrassed if they did not go along with the powerful pressures they feel to take this route. Many of them are capable of understanding that the whole idea behind today's culture is to dangle happiness out in front of people so they will keep plodding along, like a donkey with a carrot tied in front of its head, without any real end point in sight. They can see why workaholics – even those who love their jobs – are so miserable. But as cultural creatures, nothing is more unnerving than the feeling that one is a failure according to existing cultural standards. Thus many people who slave, shop, and consume their way to a counterfeit happiness are simply afraid to reject their cultural conditioning.

One of the finest definitions of happiness is the one below by British novelist Margaret Storm Jameson. Not only does it capture the key ingredients of happiness, but it refers to the need to risk oneself in order to achieve it.

Happiness Key

Happiness comes of the capacity to feel deeply, to enjoy simply, to think freely, to risk life, to be needed.

– MARGARET STORM JAMESON

In a classic episode of the television comedy *Seinfeld*, the character George Costanza lights upon the idea that he would be happier if he did everything oppositely. He tried it and, to his amazement, it worked. He was in effect experimenting with contrarianism. Some disenchanted people have already discovered that the path of contradiction has great potential for happiness.

G. K. Chesterton thought of himself as a cultural contrarian: 'I owe my success to having listened respectfully to the very best advice, and then going and doing the exact opposite.' He was also a contrarian when it came to happiness. Chesterton had an extraordinary capacity to experience a childlike wonder from ordinary life, and to use this as the basis for the 'deepest philosophy of life', as he termed it. He was utterly sceptical of claims that happiness was to be found out there somewhere in a world of material purchases and orchestrated titillations.

Chesterton could see in himself this trait that, however contrary to prevailing notions about where to find happiness, gave him the happiness of a child: 'I do not think there is anyone who takes quite such fierce pleasure in things being themselves as I do. The startling wetness of water excites and intoxicates me: the fieriness of fire, the steeliness of steel, the unutterable muddiness of mud. It is just the same with people.' The simple miracle of life itself holds all that is needed for a true happiness.

While contrarianism is not a perfect solution, one would almost certainly come out ahead in terms of happiness by moving reflexively in the opposite direction of the current cultural voice. For instance, as soon as we hear 'buy' messages, we give something away. 'Stay focused' and 'Keep your eye on the ball' means create more free time and explore neglected passions. 'You deserve it' and 'Look out for number one' means muzzling one's ego and becoming a positive role model for a vulnerable child. 'Let's shop till we drop' means finding a quiet place for spiritual reflection. 'You need a bigger car' means get a good used bicycle. 'Oh what a loser she is!' means I want to get to know her. 'Become a professional' means devote your life to amateurism and do things for the sheer love of it. Maybe we should pay tribute to the psychic waywardness of consumer culture in providing so clear a direction, albeit an opposite one, to inner happiness.

Futurists sometimes disagree that we must completely re-vamp our culture and its norms in order to stay alive to happiness, and to safeguard our survival. They speculate that continuing advances in technology are going to result in a 'transhuman happiness' that no longer has anything to do with our original natures. The World Transhumanist Association defines transhumanism as 'a philosophy which advocates the use of technology to overcome our biological limitations and transform the human condition'. Some transhumanists envision neurotechnology that would allow us to manipulate the brain's pleasure centres to enhance the quality of the emotions, and to lock us into never-ending states of happiness. They see this virtual happiness being enhanced in ways that allow us to transcend humanity, such as the eradication of all aging, disease, and infirmity.

Even if this techno-happiness were to become a reality, it would no longer be happiness in the traditional sense of the word. Being detached from the negative emotions and the periods of non-happiness that incubate happiness, it would be a one-dimensional experience devoid of all meaning outside of itself. The last thing we need is for happiness to become even less meaningful than it is today.

Research with university students in the United States shows that as many as 60 per cent of them feel as if they are in an 'existential void', a finding that is often blamed on the joint effects of consumerism and narcissism. This percentage is not quite as high among young people in Europe, but it is increasing as consumption continues to become the hub of meaning. Therefore, as a society we need to shift our educational approaches in order to attach greater value to the achievement of a meaningful life, rather than merely 'making it'. As part of this, educators must reintroduce life's 'Big Questions' into the curricula, since happiness that avoids all the big questions is no happiness at all.

Part of the challenge ahead is to promote what Canadian psychologist Richard Bucke called 'cosmic consciousness' in his 1902 book by that same title. This involves the person having a broad worldview and a high level of awareness of one's unity with the universe. Like the Eastern concept of enlightenment, it delivers a type of happiness that stems from intellectual illumination, heightened moral sensibilities, and a life founded on compassion and love. Those who are calling for a greater emphasis on 'meaningful happiness' argue similarly that true happiness depends on life philosophies that can return to us a sense that we are connected spiritually to the world and all its creatures.

In his essay 'In Search of Meaning: Some Thoughts on Belief, Doubt, and Well-being', cultural psychologist Anthony Marsella writes that belief systems and worldviews with a spiritual dimension open up new levels of awareness and help people to grow by way of awe, mystery, reverence, and transcendence. This allows the 'meaning-making process' to mature beyond the current meaning systems that are mired in materialism and consumption. Marsella speaks about the important role of doubt in being able to question critically the beliefs and values that have been injected into us through cultural indoctrination.

But what does a single individual do when confronted with the reality that his or her happiness is founded on unhealthy low-level cultural beliefs and assumptions? It is a lot to ask such people to find a type of happiness that is at direct odds with the prevailing gods of money, success, and personal pleasure.

Happiness Key

Happiness is an illusion if it does not involve making someone else happy.

JUAN ZAPATERO

Over the years, as people have become more self-centred and fixated on their personal entitlements, I find myself advising increasing numbers of my psychotherapy clients to become involved in some sort of volunteer work. The idea is that this will help take their minds off themselves while furthering the happiness and welfare of others. There are even a number of studies showing that volunteer work has the effect of enhancing happiness, while giving people a greater sense of purpose and connectedness. It also helps to lessen the disturbing loneliness that lies at the heart of the consumer experience.

One of the best means of finding happiness is to become absorbed into a cause greater than oneself. The value of self-sacrifice is a lesson that is sorely lacking from the type of education that young people are receiving today. Even if one is not always feeling happy, it is always possible to bring happiness to others, which ultimately comes back to the giver. It is sometimes said that the happiest of all people are those who plant the seeds of happiness in others, even if they will not be there to watch them grow.

Author Charles Gow once wrote that 'Many people are extremely happy, but are absolutely worthless to society.' That captures very nicely much of the happiness that we see today. However extreme it may be, it lacks sufficient humanity to register at a level that sustains the person and provides a reason for one's existence. We can only hope that, in the future, we will collectively remember that life is about much more than happiness. It is heartening to see that some visionary educators are already calling for alternative approaches that place far greater emphasis on the development of character. Without substance, a person is destined to grope for the banal happiness that lies within the pointless values that are polluting the emotions today.

It is an unfortunate reality that we live in a world that predisposes people to be depressed, stressed, hurried, materialistic, discontented, greedy, needlessly complicated, narcissistic, bored and indifferent, fearful, lonely, alienated, rageful, spiritually starved, uncharitable, under-touched, play deprived, dance deprived, sleep deprived, intellectually dull, divorced from curiosity and creativity, removed from nature, desperate for intimacy, adrift from family and friends, existentially confused, physically unfit, and enslaved to debt. Almost every aspect of the modern way of life diminishes our chances of meaningful happiness.

In the throes of this social, cultural, spiritual, and environmental holocaust, people cannot avoid the unconscious fear that they will never be happy. It is only to be expected that they would compensate by surrounding themselves with happy faces and a thousand other proofs that they are in fact happy. But in reality I believe that a heart-felt happiness is beyond the reach of most people who regard consumer culture to be their psychological home. The search for happiness has become the search for a new psychological and cultural home. Happiness may be an endangered state of mind, but at least it is a renewable resource that can stage a comeback if, as a society, we rediscover what it means to live like human beings.

DATE DUE
